AF208358

A Journey of Dreams

EVERY STRUGGLE IS A SUCCESS, AND EVERY SUCCESS HAS ITS ROOTS IN A DREAM

RAM S. VERMA

Srishti
PUBLISHERS & DISTRIBUTORS

Srishti Publishers & Distributors
A unit of AJR Publishing LLP
212A, Peacock Lane
Shahpur Jat, New Delhi – 110 049

editorial@srishtipublishers.com

First published by
Srishti Publishers & Distributors in 2024

ACKNOWLEDGMENTS

I would like to express my deepest gratitude to the people who have supported me throughout the journey of writing the book, *A Journey of Dreams*. Their encouragement, guidance, and unwavering belief in my abilities have been invaluable.

First and foremost, I want to thank my family for their unwavering support. Your love and understanding provided the foundation upon which I built this project.

A heartfelt thank you to my dedicated editor, Stuti Sharma, whose keen insights and constructive feedback significantly enhanced the quality of this manuscript. Your commitment to excellence has been instrumental in bringing this book to its fruition.

I am indebted to the beta readers of this book - my friends and colleagues who generously shared their expertise and offered valuable suggestions. Your diverse perspectives enriched the content and added depth to the narrative.

I extend my appreciation to Arup Bose and the entire team at Srishti Publishers, from the talented cover designer to the meticulous proofreaders. Your dedication to bringing this book to life is truly commendable.

Lastly, to the readers who will embark on this literary adventure, thank you for your time and curiosity. Writing is a solitary endeavor, but it is the readers who give meaning to the words on these pages.

This book would not have been possible without the collective support of these incredible individuals. I am profoundly grateful for each and every one of you.

PART 01

The Excursion

THE FIRST FLIGHT

On the afternoon of 29th July 2007, a tall, narrow-shouldered young man in his early thirties was standing in the queue at the check-in counter of Air Korea at Terminal 2 of Chhatrapati Shivaji Maharaj International Airport, Mumbai, India and waiting for his turn to receive the boarding pass. He was well-dressed and his curly hair and short beard distinguished him from the crowd, but his eyes that were scanning every corner, made him noticeable.

He was bewildered by his surroundings. Wiping the dried perspiration from his reddened face, he sniffed at his shirt.

The queue was long, but he was comfortable staying where he was, as waiting in line gave him time to observe the others, learn how to check-in on a flight and look around the splendid airport inside. He held his documents ready in hand. He waited for about fifteen minutes, often checking his passport, balancing a file and some papers in his hand while constantly observing the others.

"Next, please," requested the attendant at Counter No. 2.

It was Anubhav's turn to move on and he stepped forward immediately.

"Good afternoon, madam!" He looked carefully at the name tag pinned on her blazer. 'Hannah', he could read her name as he came up to the counter.

"Good evening, sir," she responded with a flawless smile. "How are you doing today?"

Then, extending her hand towards the gentleman, she asked, "May I have your passport, please?"

Anubhav had heard that the smile of the attendants was usually fake, since it was a requirement of the business. However, he found himself to be mistaken. Her smile appeared genuine and was as pretty as her elegant, glamorous and cheerful appearance.

"Thank you for asking," he said, while courteously handing over his passport and documents. "I am doing very well today."

There was silence for about three minutes, broken only by the clicking of the keyboard. Anubhav looked at her, while her eyes were glued to the computer screen.

"Can I get a window seat, please?" Anubhav requested, looking questioningly at the lady.

"I will check for it, sir," said the employee, taking her eyes off the computer screen and looking at him. "Can you please put your bags on for weighing?"

There was silence once again. The lady checked his documents, verified the details and weighed both his bags.

Then, she became busy, completing entries on her computer. Unexpectedly, she said, "Sir, you have already selected a window seat." She smiled at him and asked, "Do you want a different seat?"

"No, no... I want the same seat," Anubhav responded instantly. "Please don't change it."

Although he had selected a window seat online soon after booking his flight ticket, he wanted to ensure that he would get one.

The boarding pass was ready, and handing it to him, the flight attendant said, "Sir, these are your boarding passes. Would you mind proceeding to Gate No. 14?"

"Sure. Thank you, madam."

He remained standing there and looked at the passes carefully. There were two boarding passes – one was from Mumbai to Seoul and the other, from Seoul to San Francisco. It was a connecting flight and no other check-in was required.

"Have a wonderful journey!" said the lady, not receiving any further response from the passenger.

"Thank you, madam," he acknowledged once again and moved towards Gate No. 14 to board the flight.

He walked cautiously while following the sign boards and looked around the airport with his mouth open. This was not Anubhav's first visit to this airport. He came here occasionally to bid farewell to his friends and colleagues travelling overseas for business and tours. Each time he came to see anyone off, a question would come into his mind as to when would it be his turn, and would he have the fortune to board a flight?

Fortune had smiled at him. He was going to board the first flight of his life and that too, an international flight! Everything was new to him – from stepping inside, the baggage check-in and receiving a boarding pass to take a flight. He was amazed at the magnificence and excellence of the interior of the airport, and its grandeur couldn't have been imagined without being present there.

After passing through the security check, he noticed 'Flight KE656: Mumbai to Seoul' written on the display board. The gate at the back was locked and the flight crew was preparing to board. The passengers were sitting in chairs on both sides of the gate, waiting for the door to open.

Anubhav was travelling to San Francisco, CA and it was a connecting flight. The connecting flight was ten hours later from Seoul. He looked at both the boarding passes again, matched the flight number displayed on the gate and assured himself that he was in the right place. Then, he took a seat and looked around the waiting area.

There was silence and the passengers sat on benches without stirring or speaking, though he saw a great deal that was strange and funny.

A six-year-old boy was sitting next to him with his mother. When a lame man came into the waiting area, limping on one leg, the boy wanted to hop too. He nudged his mother's elbow, giggled in his sleeve and said, "Look, Mummy, a sparrow."

"Hush, Titu, hush!" said his mother.

The boy turned towards Anubhav, who was looking at him and grinning. Both of them smiled and waved at each other.

Soon, there was an announcement.

"Passengers travelling to Seoul, please start boarding."

The boarding began and passengers were permitted to move through the gate, one after the other. Anubhav joined the queue, along with the funny lad who had hopped, Titu, and his mother.

Finally, he could see the plane clearly as he walked ahead through the gate. While he was walking, he used his fingertips to calculate in his mind, how many days, months and years he had prayed and struggled sorely for this miracle to happen.

As he neared the door of the airplane, two beautiful air hostesses dressed in celadon business formals stood there.

"How many times will they check the passport and ticket?" he thought, looking at them, though he had all his documents handy.

"Good morning, sir," welcomed both flight attendants, bowing slightly as he approached the gate. "Welcome to Air Korea!"

No one had greeted Anubhav like this before. He bowed down as well and nodded at both of them. Looking at the young passenger, the calm expressions on their faces vanished and were replaced with broad grins. One of the air hostesses took his boarding pass, checked the seat number marked on it and then, guided him as to where his seat was and the line moved on.

"I should not have bowed down," thought Anubhav. Embarrassed, he dropped his eyes to the floor and moved forward. Titu, who was behind him in line, followed his example and bowed in a similar manner. Anubhav was on a flight for the first time in his life. Happiness, anxiety and fear caught at him at once and he didn't know how he reached row number thirty-five. He sat down in the window seat of this row, and looking outside, he saw a world that looked familiar.

He came back to his senses to some degree and continued to minutely scrutinize every movement inside the aircraft and eyeing everyone who crossed him. He stood up from his seat abruptly, and hearing a plaintive voice, turned to look backwards. He arched his back to see what was wrong; it was Titu in the back seat on his mother's lap, refusing to go to his seat and fasten the seat belt. They both looked at each other and waved their hands again, beaming.

Anubhav's co-passenger turned his face to the right, looking upwards at him, screwing up his eyes. He was looking intently at him. His face looked angry, ill-tempered and preoccupied, like that of a man in pain who was being forced to listen to nonsense. Anubhav looked at him and dropped his eyes at once. A strange, cautious look appeared on his face and he was back in his seat.

He dropped his eyes to a magazine placed in the pocket of the back of the seat in front of him. He remained quiet for two minutes, even though it seemed to him as if every vein in his body was quivering and fluttering with pleasure. Slowly, he raised his head, craned his neck and peeped outside the window.

With a noise of the engine, the aircraft started rolling towards the runway at a crawling speed that was slower than that of a bicycle. Anubhav was holding his breath and his heart started beating faster. Once again, his curiosity gained the better of his pretended dignity. His eyelids began fluttering to seize every minute of the most exciting moment of his life. The speed of the aircraft increased, and he was about to scream.

Unexpectedly, the plane turned towards the right and its acceleration stopped as soon as it turned. The aircraft was now standing on the main runway and the tall trees at a distance, enclosed within a razor wire fence alongside the long grey wall, stopped moving. Anubhav managed to stop himself from screaming, thinking how ugly it would have been. He didn't know why the plane stood mid-way, but just then, he heard an announcement.

"Good afternoon, passengers. This is Joe and I am the captain of your flight. Firstly, I welcome everyone on board Air Korea flight KE656 from New Delhi to Seoul. We are currently second in line for take off and expect to be in the air in around five minutes."

Anubhav listened carefully, although he was busy looking at the scene outside the window. The plane was standing in the middle of the runway. Its engines were as silent as though their fire had been extinguished. The airport was surrounded by a six feet high grey concrete boundary wall that was visible from the runway. The wall was two hundred yards from the runway and broken at one point. The razor wire fence on top of it was missing at the broken part. A few children could be seen climbing over the half-broken wall, watching the flights takeoff off with whooping and cheering. The structure loomed dark against the lighter horizon, due to which, their appearance was blurred and not clear. An inspection of the grass and surrounding bushes yielded no results, but that of the broken boundary wall provided him with many valuable clues. It did not require much of an effort on Anubhav's part to distinguish one face among them.

A thought flashed through his mind at once as he recalled a boy sitting on a similar airport boundary wall, alone and lost in his thoughts. His curiosity and excitement about boarding his first flight and witness its take-off suddenly waned. The pictures of his past flashed before his eyes faster than the accelerating plane. Closing his eyes, he took a few deep breaths and started reminiscing about the past.

Five minutes had passed and the aeroplane's speed broke the sound barrier and lifted off the ground. Anubhav had waited for years for this moment to come in his life, but a past memory overshadowed his excitement and the noise of the newest Rolls-Royce 267 KN twin-engine of the plane changed to a long whistle of a train that sounded repeatedly while departing from Satna railway station towards Mumbai.

2

A RESTLESS JOURNEY

It was the summer of July 2003 and Anubhav was sitting in the sleeper compartment number S9 of the Mahanagari Express to Mumbai. The train had just departed from Satna railway station, from where he had boarded it and was slowly gaining speed. It was drizzling outside, so the passengers pulled down their window panes as the train left the platform, but it didn't capture his attention, though he was constantly staring out of the window. There was continuous lightning, but he could hear no thunder. It was only when he heard a tone, edged with displeasure did he realize that others were sitting there too.

"Hey, young man, can't you see that it's raining?" said an old man angrily, who was sitting beside him. "Do you want to make all of us sick? Close the window!"

Anubhav turned towards the window and closed it, but he was lost once again in his thoughts.

A train journey held great appeal, especially in the rainy season. However, it didn't appeal to the young boy, and he did not look like any other passenger. A tormented thought was haunting and crushing him horribly, robbing him of peace for many days and nights.

He had left home and was travelling in search of a dream job. He knew it was not going to be easy, and this journey was going to decide his destiny and what he would become in his life. His mind was filled with questions that were electrifying, and he did not know the answer to any of them. Only destiny knew whether the journey would lead to success or failure. Anubhav knew it would be the most unpredictable and arduous journey of his life, and he had no clue as to how many days it would last. This feeling of uncertainty had given rise to an oppressive dread of what would come next.

The train was still moving slowly. Seeing that the old man had fallen asleep, he opened the window slowly. A mild, cold breeze was blowing outside and came in through the open window, accompanied by the mist and raindrops. The droplets spattering inside were hitting him and spraying his face. This mist sowed the seeds of a dream that he had for years.

Two months ago in May 2003, his final semester examinations had concluded. The Khalsa Institute of Technology, Jabalpur, was an average engineering college with no placement opportunities. All his classmates had decided their next steps before the final semester exams were over and had a plan in place. Almost everyone was moving out of Jabalpur and migrating to other cities, wherever job opportunities existed. Some planned to pursue higher studies and had appeared in the entrance exams. They were waiting for the results. A few had enrolled in coaching classes and were eager to attend a top-ranking college for higher education. The rest of them planned to enroll in popular professional courses and training in the job market.

Jabalpur was not an IT city and didn't conform to the dream of a graduate in software engineering, so almost all of his friends were leaving one after the other for future endeavours. No one was going back to their native place. Instead, they were all going to metropolitan cities such as Pune, Delhi, or Bangalore, where IT professionals were in high demand.

Anubhav stayed back, watching everyone leave the hostel and city for good. He went to the railway station each time anyone was moving out, helped them board the train, hugged them one last time and saw them off. Everyone said goodbye when they left and Anubhav would walk back alone to the same hostel room. Upon reaching his room, he would have a million questions in his mind about what he should do next. He had completed his education in very challenging circumstances and had managed to finish it. But now, he had to move to a new city to get a job.

He could go to a city where the cost of living was high, only if he could ensure free accommodation and two meals a day. He was tortured by the thought of returning to his village, and his nights became more oppressive than ever with each passing day.

All his roommates and friends left Jabalpur within two weeks of the final exams. The noisy hostel became barren, and he was left all alone, still looking for an opportunity. The allotment of the hostel room was only till the end of the month and the mess would also close by then as there was nobody left besides him. Anubhav spent the weeks in solitude and had yet to decide on a path ahead. At last, he had no choice but to return to his village. He packed his bags and left for his village on the day that the hostel mess closed.

He reached Birpur, his village, towards the evening. In his memories, he had painted his home as a bright, snug and comfortable one. In reality, it was a mud house with two enclosures and a wide veranda-type living room, having two little windows on both sides of the old, stiff door and was surrounded by a well-aligned reed fence.

As he approached the hut, he felt positively frightened. It was dark inside and very crowded as well as unclean. It looked as though the hut was about to fall to pieces. In the corner, facing the door, bundles of maize were stacked against the wall and a grocery bag was hanging. A clothesline had been hung using two pegs and there were pictures of gods and goddesses pegged on it. Dirty clothes were swinging on another twine that was stretched from one end of the room to the other. An earthen brick stove was on the other side, with flies buzzing around it. Poverty could be seen in every corner of the hut.

An eight-year-old black-haired girl was sitting near the brick stove, unwashed and apathetic. A white dog was lying on the floor with his eyes closed. She glanced at Anubhav as he came in and ran towards him, exclaiming, "Elder brother!"

The dog opened his eyes simultaneously and ran towards him too. Beating the girl, it jumped at him, licking him and wagging his tail.

"Sheru! Oh, Sheru!" exclaimed the newcomer. "Come on… stop it!"

"He bites," warned the little girl. "He bit a boy last week."

"How is that? When did he start biting?"

"He was beaten by a group of boys," informed the little girl. "He bit one of them."

With the first glance, Anubhav remembered what life was like. He put down his bags in silence and went out of the house into the village street. This hut was the third from the end of the lane and seemed to be the poorest and oldest of them all; the next was similar to it but the last one had brick walls, a tiled roof and curtains in the windows. All the huts stood in a row and the whole village looked serene and captivating. With ponds full of lotus flowers, fruit trees peeping from the yards and elderly people sitting in the doorways, the village had an engaging look.

Above the farmlands, there was a slope down to the river. Winding paths ran down the hill along the gravel and holes dug by the potters.

Bits of broken ceramic in red and brown, lay piled up in heaps and a broad, level, sunny, green meadow stretched below it. The hay had been already been cut and cattle were grazing in it. The river twisted and turned with beautiful, leafy banks about two miles from the village. Above it, there was another vast meadow, another herd of cattle, long rows of white pigeons and a primary school at some distance. Then, there was a steep path uphill and a little temple on top of the hill.

Just at that moment, the bells began to toll. Two young girls with water pitchers on their heads looked towards the temple to listen to the hymns being sung.

'At this time, the village market should be lively and full, but it must be lovely at the bank of the river,' thought Anubhav, dreamily.

Sitting on the edge of the slope of the hill, he watched the sunset. The crimson and gold sky reflected in the river, the temple top and the entire atmosphere was so soothing, calm and virginal as though it wasn't Jabalpur at all. When the sunlight faded, flocks of birds flew across the sky and herds of cattle ambled along the way, bleating and lowing. Pigeons flew across the river and everything plunged into silence. The soft light disappeared and dusk set in.

Meanwhile, Anubhav's father and mother – two gaunt, bent, toothless, aged people of the same height, who had been working on the farms beyond the river, arrived home. Anubhav went inside the hut and saw his parents, grandparents as well as five brothers and sisters.

"Where is Manubhav?" he asked, after touching their feet and greeting them. His youngest brother was not present there.

"He has gone to Uncle's village," answered his father. "Work on a road has started there."

"He is working on a road? What about his school?"

"He is no longer going to school. We can't afford the fees," said his grandfather, a toothless old man. "He is not interested in studying like you. He failed in three subjects."

"But grandpa..." Anubhav heaved a sigh, realizing he had made a mistake in coming here instead of working somewhere in Jabalpur.

After a few hours, the family assembled on the covered verandah, waiting to start dinner. All the men including Anubhav Gumrah, his father Diwakar Gumrah, grandfather Prabhakar Gumrah and two younger brothers – Sanju and Manu, sat on square wooden planks. While his eldest sister, Manju, was assisting her mother in serving the food, the eighth and youngest sister, Minu, was sitting with her grandmother next to the clay stove, which was still burning, though its smoke had filled the house.

Anubhav kept exchanging glances with his mother as he ate dinner. He laid down his morsel several times and cleared his throat, as if meaning to say something, but after looking at his father, he would continue eating. At last, when the *payasam* had been served, he cleared his throat and said hesitantly:

"I want to go to any metropolis like Bangalore or Pune to look for a job. All my friends have moved there. I should have gone earlier; I have wasted a fortnight."

"Well, go, why are you loafing around here? You should be earning by now. Pack up and go," the father asserted bluntly. "Good luck to you."

Everybody looked down at their plates and a minute passed in silence.

"He needs money to live," his mother said in a low voice.

"Money? Are you sure you can't do anything without money?" said his father. "Take everything I have. You could have taken it long ago!"

Anubhav heaved a faint sigh and looked uneasily at his mother.

"How much do you want?" questioned his father, when the boy didn't reply.

"I need the fare to the city and it is likely to take some time for me to find work. I need to ask you for five thousand rupees."

"Ah, money, always money!" sighed his father. "What is left now? My farms have already been mortgaged to pay for your college education."

Diwakar thought for some time and then heaved a sigh.

"You will have to manage on your own now. I have done what I could for you," said his father in an angry tone.

Like all mothers, Anubhav's mother, lacking in prudence and diplomacy, could not restrain herself and said, "You ought to give him a few thousand rupees more. How will he go to a new city and look for a job?"

No sooner had she spoken these words that a storm broke out.

Anubhav's father's short, thin neck turned as red as a beetroot. The colour spread slowly to his ears and then to his temples and suffused his whole face by degrees. His father shifted position and unbuttoned his shirt collar to save himself from choking. He was struggling with a feeling that was engulfing him. A deathlike silence followed, and the children held their breath. His mother went on, as though she did not understand what was happening to her husband:

"You know that he is not a little boy now. He understands what he needs to do."

"Take everything!" Anubhav's father shouted in a strange voice. "Loot me! Take it all! Strangle me!" An expression of anger, resentment and deprivation was writ large on his face.

He jumped up from his seat, clutched his head and ran staggering around the room.

"Strip me to the last thread!" he shouted shrilly. "Squeeze out the last drop! Rob me! Wring my neck!"

Anubhav flushed and dropped his eyes. He could not continue to eat. His mother, who had not grown used to her husband's complex character even after thirty years, shrank into herself and muttered something in self-defence. Her pale and bird-like face which always looked soft and scared, now showed shock and suppressed terror. The little boys and the elder daughter Manju, a girl in her teens with a pale, ugly face, stood mute with tears in their eyes.

Diwakar was growing more and more angry and uttering words, each more terrible than the ones before. He said, "I have sold everything for you!"

Anubhav turned pale and stood up. "Listen papa," he began, gasping for breath, "I... I beg you to end this, for..."

"Hold your tongue!" cried his father, and he stamped his feet. "You must listen to what I say! Hold your tongue. At your age, I was earning my living while you... Do you know what you have cost me, you scoundrel?"

"Please calm down; he has come today only. At least, let him eat," muttered his mother, wringing her hands nervously. "You know him... you know!"

"Hold your tongue!" Diwakar shouted at her and tears of anger filled his eyes. "He came back without a job. I sold everything for him. From where should I get more money?"

The daughter Minu gazed fixedly at her mother with her mouth open, turned pale and uttering a loud shriek, fell back on the floor. Anubhav's father ran out into the yard, cursing and waving his hands around. The aged man, Prabhakar, finished his food without any reaction, as if nothing had happened.

This was how domestic scenes usually ended at his home. However, on this occasion, Anubhav was unfortunately swept away by his overpowering anger. He was just as hasty and ill-tempered as his father and grandfather, who had once beaten a labourer almost to death with a stick. Clenching his fists, Anubhav went to his mother and shouted in the highest pitch that his voice could reach:

"These reproaches are loathsome and sicken me! I want nothing from you! Nothing! I would rather die of hunger than eat another bite at your expense!"

His mother huddled against the door and wrung her hands. "What have I done?" she wailed. "What?"

Like his father, the boy shook his hands and ran into the yard. Then, he walked along the muddy road towards the open country with the dog following him. The air was full of dampness due to the rain. The road was muddy with puddles formed here and there and the grass in the green fields looked dismal, decaying and dark. On the right side of the road were vegetable gardens that looked gloomy, with tomatoes and other leafy vegetables growing.

Anubhav thought that it would be a good idea to walk to Pune or Bangalore, just as he was – without boots, proper clothes or a single rupee. When he would have travelled ten miles, his father, scared and horrified, would overtake him and beg him to turn back or take money, but he would not even look at him and instead, would go on and on. Dense forests would be followed by deserted fields and then, the forest again. Soon, somewhere near a jungle, he would fall down exhausted and starving, and die. His remains would be found only if not eaten by wild animals and there would be a news item in all the newspapers saying that an aspiring engineer had died of hunger.

He walked along the road and thought of death, the suffering of his family, the misery of his father. He imagined all sorts of adventures on the road, each more exquisite than the one before, involving scenic places, difficult nights and chance encounters.

He imagined a series of pilgrims and a hut in the woodland, with one tiny window through which a light shimmered in the darkness. He imagined himself standing in front of the window and begging for a night's shelter. The dwellers let him in and soon, he sees that they are bandits; or better still, he is taken into a big landlord's house, whereupon learning who he is, they offer him food and drink, play to him on the piano, listen to his heartaches and the beautiful daughter of the house falls in love with him.

Lost in his bitterness and such reflections, Anubhav strode on and on. Far ahead, he saw an inn, a dark patch against the gray background of the clouds. Further on from the inn, near the horizon, he could see a little hillock. The railway station was on this hillock. It reminded him of the distance between where he was now standing and Pune and Bangalore, where street lamps glowed, cars and motors rattled in the streets and he worked in a big multinational company as a software engineer. He almost wept with dismay and impatience. Despite its order and magnificence, the solemn terrain and deathlike stillness all around, revolted him and caused him to feel anguish and self-hatred.

Anubhav walked along the road till dark, immersed in dreary thoughts. Suddenly, it began to drizzle. He turned back and looked at the dog that was still following him with his tongue out and breathing fast.

"Oh, Sheru... Sheru," he said and bending down, hugged and kissed the dog. Then, he turned back towards home and said, "Let's go home."

PART 2

The Strife of an Insolvent

3

REACHING THE PROMISED LAND

Two weeks had passed since Anubhav had returned to the village and he was becoming more heartbroken with each passing day. One day, one of his relatives visited their house. He served in the Army Medical Corps. Anubhav learned that he had been transferred to Pune and was on his way to join the Cardiac Therapy Center (MH-CTC) at the military hospital. Anubhav's father had invited him to visit them.

Looking at Anubhav's tense face, the visitor said, "I am an army personnel and don't know anything about engineering and the IT industry. So, I cannot help you get a job, but you can live with me and look for one."

A shining ray of hope shone between his throbbing temples. Fascinated by his uncle's words, he ran inside his room to get a pen and paper and noted his address as well as contact details in his diary.

A week later, at around six o'clock in the morning, a rickshaw was waiting for him outside his home. He said goodbye to all his family affectionately and even shed a few tears. As he passed his father's room, he glanced in at the door and stood by the little window, drumming his fingers on the pane.

"I am leaving," said the son.

"Goodbye. The money is under your pillow," his father answered, without turning around.

The boy went outside and while sitting on the rickshaw, he looked in the cowshed outside the house. Both their bulls were missing.

"Mother, where are our bulls?" he asked, in a shaky voice.

Ignoring her son's question and with tears in her eyes, his mother waved and said, "Goodbye, my son. May success be with you."

After a journey of more than twenty-four hours, a sleepless night and a change-over to another train at Kalyan Junction, Anubhav arrived at the Pune railway station. As soon as he came outside the station, he looked at the blue sky and the sun that was still dull enough to be looked at. The earth was refreshed with the sun-kissed dew, and the fresh air was filled with the sounds of rapture and hope.

"What wonderful weather!" he exclaimed. "What an atmosphere!"

An auto-rickshaw rolled over towards him and the driver asked him invitingly, "Sir, where do you want to go?"

"MH-CTC, before Wanwadi Bazaar," the young gentleman answered, pretending as though he was not new to the city.

He arranged the bags in the rear of the auto-rickshaw. A beggar approached him at the same time, waving his hand towards him. Anubhav put a two rupee coin in his hand, wishing that those two rupees would atone for his mistakes and safeguard his home with the blessings of god. The traveller boarded the auto-rickshaw, and it started running towards the cantonment area of the city with an uninterrupted speed in the sparse early morning traffic.

"Sir, are you going to the hospital or the family quarters?" the driver asked his passenger, as he sat quietly, deep in thought.

"Oh... I need to go to the family quarters. My uncle serves in the hospital but stays in the hospital staff quarters." Anubhav gave the driver the complete address of where he had to go.

Soon, the auto-rickshaw stopped by a boom gate and an extremely fit and slender sentry, dressed in green and tan camouflage stepped forward.

"Where are you going? This is the staff's gate."

Leaning outside and showing the address in his diary, Anubhav said, "I am here to visit Havaldar R.K. Chauhan."

"Oh, so you are not a patient. Chauhan sir lives in C block of the new buildings," said the sentry, pointing out the direction to follow and opening the gate.

The auto-rickshaw drove in at a slower pace. The road was wide enough for another vehicle to pass and a few pedestrians were walking along it.

After going less than half a mile, the driver braked, and the auto-rickshaw came to a stop near a freshly whitewashed building. There was a small garden with lily bushes that were covered with construction dust. The lime smell of paint was still in the air.

It was easy to locate his uncle's quarters. A name plate was hanging outside the first house at the lower level – Havaldar R.K. Chauhan, Nursing Assistant. Anubhav identified it quickly. His uncle, a non-commissioned officer, had been transferred recently and worked in the department of cardiology. He lived in the staff family quarters with his wife and two small kids, aged six and three years old.

After the nightmarish days since the closing of the college, Anubhav had no choice but to go back to the village where poverty and misery were the only fortune. He wished to go to any IT city and fate had chosen this city for him. Pune was the most popular city for a software engineering graduate, besides Bangalore and Hyderabad.

The delightful present was blended with the impressions of the past that stirred within him. There was a strange fear in his heart; yet he was happy.

He exclaimed in awe, "Anubhav, you have reached the gateway to your dreams. It's not an ordinary city, but a promised land that God has chosen for you!"

A day passed and brimming with enthusiasm, Anubhav was raring to go out in search of a job, but he didn't know where to go or how to start.

The next day, Anubhav joined his uncle when he came for lunch and visited his workplace at the hospital. It would not lead to a path to take him to the door of an IT company, but it could be a starting point for becoming familiar with the city and its whereabouts.

MH-CTC was a big hospital and the cardiology department was its primary division. Anubhav met the medical practitioners there and the staff working with his uncle. After spending an hour with his uncle in his nursing room, he roamed around throughout the hospital, eyeing and exploring every part of it.

The Military Hospital (Cardio Therapy Centre), commonly known as MH-CTC, located in Wanwadi Bazaar, a part of the Pune cantonment area, was established in 1945 as the Indo-British General Hospital in Pune. It had emerged as a leading tertiary care super-specialty centre. The hospital was committed to providing comprehensive, holistic patient care for pulmonary tuberculosis and cardiac and respiratory diseases, to retired as well as serving soldiers and their families.

Though Pune was a big city with high-rise buildings near each other, the hospital was located in a remarkably peaceful and quiet part of the city with an abundance of greenery and having a small hill behind it. The ground had sawdust and gravel scattered around and the trees had hard and knotted trunks, worn smooth with time, unlike any other part of the city.

Patients and staff in hospital liveries and visitors were walking around and while following them, he discovered a new place. An amphitheatre was located behind the hospital, towards the hill. It was a garden with a variety of flowers and plants where patients could be seen relaxing in the sun, away from the main building.

He heard the evening prayer bell ring when he followed a trail back towards the quarters that were midway between the hospital administrative block and the residential section. By now, the sun was setting behind Baner Hill and the air was redolent with the smell of freshly cut grass that was still wet. The spire of a temple shone in the dwindling sunlight and patients, families, and a few soldiers in uniform walked towards the gate. He followed them.

On reaching the temple courtyard, he removed his shoes, washed his feet at the nearby fountain, splashed water on his perspiring face and then entered the temple, ringing the bell loudly at the entrance. He knelt on the ground, and joining his hands together, prayed to god to show him the path, fulfill the purpose of his journey and bring his family out of poverty and grief.

He pledged to offer food service in the temple when he got a job, wash dirty dishes, donate a part of his salary to the poor and distribute blankets to beggars. He stood for five minutes in silence with his eyes closed before Lord Krishna's idol.

Suddenly, two big drops of tears fell from his eyes, rolling down his cheeks. He was thinking about the two bulls. He vowed to buy a tractor for his father once he started earning and to bring both the bulls that his father had pledged, back from the wicked merchant.

4

PREPARING FOR A RACE

A week passed without any meaningful action. Visiting the temple in the morning, touring the hospital and meeting the medical staff, and patients became his routine. The staff was humble and cooperative but their field was medicine and no one knew anything about the IT industry or how to approach for a job in it. Being a military hospital, everyone served there for a limited tenure of three to five years and so, no one had any idea of the city's IT companies, locations and software job opportunities.

He realized that he would learn about medicine by going to the hospital daily but would never become a software engineer and so, he decided to explore. After going to the hospital and picking up his uncle's Atlas bicycle, he started roaming around outside the hospital, cycling the whole day and exploring the city. Down the road to the east was a typical cantonment market called Wanwadi Bazaar and opposite this to the west, a smaller market called Mira Bazaar. Military establishments and the command hospital were on the other side, with fewer civilian vehicular movement on nearby roads.

Soon, he discovered places relevant to him, like nearby bus stops with connectivity to the city, post offices, bookstores, internet cafes, and telephone booths. Most importantly, he found a newspaper vendor near the Goliber Maidan bus stop, opposite Mira market. It was about one and a half miles from the family quarters and there was a bus stop next to it. This bus stop was about three miles from the city's central MG Road bus depot, where buses were available to any part of the city.

Anubhav noticed that the newspaper vendor would sit there for only part of the day, so he stopped by and asked for a copy of The Times of India (TOI) and asked, "What time do you open? I don't see you in the evening."

"From seven o'clock in the morning till noon every day," replied the vendor, giving him a copy of the newspaper, "you will always find me, be it rain or cold."

Anubhav knew that job openings were published in this leading newspaper. There were dedicated editorial pages called Times Ascent with it. The Times Ascent was a weekly supplement to the newspaper published on Wednesdays, focusing on human resource development, employment and job opportunities. This weekly editorial was exactly what Anubhav was looking for, in order to gain information on job postings.

Seeing this newspaper, Anubhav was confident that he could reach out to recruiters and find job opportunities. However, since it was a Saturday, he needed to wait for four more days to get a copy of the Times Ascent.

The following Wednesday, he woke up sometime between six a.m. and seven a.m. He flung on his clothes, hurriedly combed his hair and ran quickly out to the verandah. Then, he moved stealthily and went outside in the same clothes. He rushed with excitement to buy the newspaper. The traffic had just started on the roads and he abruptly and dangerously crossed the streets. He stopped by the newspaper stand after a fast walk of fifteen minutes.

It was not yet seven o'clock, but Mustafa's shop was already open. It was a small stall at one side of the road, just before the Goliber Maidan bus stop. It was half on the sidewalk and shabby. The vendor himself was an unwashed, greasy but foppishly dressed man of around forty and was busy setting up. There was nothing that required much effort but he was sweating due to his exertions.

"TOI, please," Anubhav gasped breathlessly, handing the vendor a five rupee coin, which he had already taken out of his pocket and kept in hand, halfway in his flight. The TOI's daily news editorial was priced at rupees 2.50, but Wednesday's edition cost rupees 3.50. Still, it was the cheapest newspaper and the best source of information in the country.

Mustafa gave him a copy of the newspaper. Anubhav flicked through it to check and ensure that the copy of the Ascent was along with it.

"Here is the remaining money," said the seller, raising his hand to return the balance.

"Ok, it's ok..." declined Anubhav, signalling to keep the change back in his box. "Please keep it with you."

Anubhav understood that this street vendor could be helpful to him and he wanted him to remember his face. A tip would build the first impression.

Grabbing the newspaper, Anubhav walked back at double speed, dodging the traffic and jumping a red light at a signal. Reaching home, he looked through the supplementary section – the Times Ascent first.

The weekly editorial was full of job-related articles and job postings in all fields: IT, manufacturing, pharmaceuticals and many others. He had been craving this information about job opportunities for the last two weeks. His eyes stopped at a job posting with the heading, 'Walk in – Trainee Software Engineer' at Vision Technologies. This was the first he had heard of this company. The walk-in interview was scheduled for Saturday for a 2003 pass-out engineering graduate only.

His decision to move out of the village was fruitful. He had found an opportunity for an interview in less than a month after coming to Pune.

The following Saturday, he got ready in the morning and walked to the Goliber Maidan bus stop. Vision Technologies was located in Viman Nagar. As he reached the newspaper stall, he gazed at the vendor sweeping and hitting the newspaper bundles with a scrap of a towel and they exchanged a smile.

He asked the vendor, "Bro, do you know how to reach Viman Nagar?"

"Take any bus to MG Road bus depot and change to another bus at the second bus stop," responded the seller, stopping his work and smiling back at him. "All buses go towards Viman Nagar from the second stop there."

"Thank you! I appreciate it," said the young man and then he walked to the bus stand, waiting for the next bus.

The interview was scheduled between 10:00 a.m. to 4:00 p.m., but he reached the venue before time. Thousands of applicants had already assembled outside the office building and hundreds were joining the crowd every minute. He was shocked to see such a huge gathering. He did not know that there were so many job seekers and understood the gravity of the competition for the first time. It was a scene that he had never imagined before.

Indeed, he had learned that software engineers were in high demand and they got a job easily. The reality looked very different. Anubhav felt his stomach turn and his heart went cold, while the heart itself throbbed and stood still with terror before the unknown. He could not move further. The rosy-faced fellow turned white with terror and his eyes looked for a place to hide.

All at once, he saw an isolated place at a corner of the building and walked towards it with quick steps. Not everybody could see him in there. While standing there, he observed the crowd. His perspiring body started sweating even more. He needed to ask someone where to go and what to do next.

He noticed that an HR representative was collecting resumes from the candidates near the office entrance, which he had not realized before. Everyone was going to him, but what they said was not audible. Anubhav wanted to go to the representative too, but was fearful, thinking he might be questioned.

He gathered the courage and slowly moved towards him. When he came closer to the HR representative, he heard him asking for a copy of the resume. His fear receded a little, and he moved forward with a copy.

The HR representative took a copy of his resume with the others.

"You are in batch eight," informed the HR representative and penned a number on his resume and noted some information from it in his register.

The written test had not started yet and the first batch was called inside the building. Anubhav returned to the same place behind a pillar, still sweating and thinking about what would happen next. The candidates were still arriving in large numbers and there was no place left to stand. Looking at the large number of competitors, he resigned himself to the fact that he would not be selected. Everybody in the crowd looked more competent and more intelligent than him.

The first timer considered running away out of panic, but the written test of the first batch had started and the main gate of the building was closed. A cold sweat broke out on his forehead and his body shivered. Scared of being noticed, he repeated a Sanskrit mantra in his mind, in a desperate attempt to anchor himself and remain calm.

Anubhav composed himself to face the challenge and waited for his turn, but unfortunately, he didn't get an opportunity to write the exam. An HR representative came out at 4:00 p.m. and declared that since there had been many more candidates than expected, it was not possible to continue with the remaining candidates.

"We will call the rest of the candidates next week for the test," he stated, directing them to come another day.

Without a second thought and not even waiting for the announcement to be completed, he turned and sprinted away.

Anubhav had learned that graduates of computer engineering get a job before passing out of college, which was why he had opted for it, but that did not happen with him. In contrast, he was one in a crowd of thousands of contenders. It was a fierce competition, and he needed to introspect. He slowed down as he reached outside the building. He did not want to return to the quarter and his steps were hesitant and burdened with the weight of failure.

It was five o'clock in the evening and he was walking along the road. The day was still and sultry. Feathery white clouds passed overhead and patches of shining blue sky peeped out from between them. The clouds stood motionless as though they were caught in the roofs of the tall buildings. While walking, Anubhav unexpectedly heard quick, loud thumps, and a repeated whooshing noise in the air. Shadowing his eyes from the sun with one hand and holding up his slipping backpack with the other, he gazed up at the sky. His face beamed as a giant bird passed above him.

Pune airport was alongside the road and he saw a large plane taking off in the sky. Beside the wide road, a formidable six-foot wall stood like a silent sentinel, with its stones weathered by time. As he walked along the road and reached a stray place, he discovered that the wall was broken in one place and he could glimpse inside the airport. The top of the wall was fenced using razor wire and entangled with the broken bits.

The weather was that of a beautiful August evening. The sun turned to a golden background, lightly flecked with purple and stood above the western horizon, ready to sink behind a faraway hill. On the wall by the side of the road, shadows and half-shadows had disappeared, and the air had grown damp and heavy. A golden light was still playing on the treetops.

He stood on top of the broken wall with the wind tousling his hair and could see a panoramic view that stretched till the old trees beyond the fence, vast grass fields, a runway not more than a hundred metres away and the tower at a distance. He could see the entire airport.

Suddenly, 'Boom, boom, boom!' roared through the air and a giant bird took off in the sky. After ten minutes, this sound was repeated. This persistent sound thrilled his heart and quickened his heartbeat. He had seen a plane on television and in movies before, but seeing it on an airfield was new to him. It was so close to him that he could read the letters inscribed on it and the carrier's name.

He was watching, amazed and counting how many planes took off. Abruptly, his eyes went to a nearby tree, where some weaver birds had built their nests. His eyes rested on a half-built nest in which a bird was intricately weaving strand after strand of ordinary grass.

He thought of the weaver bird. The Almighty created the weaver with its incredible ability to build an artistic nest. If a person wants to become a builder, a weaver or a craftsman, he must study and develop into one. A person must learn almost everything; fortune or destitution may come as it may, but skill comes through learning.

He also needed to build a nest that would be artistic as well as safe and protect him and his family from rain, inclement weather and any dangers. At first, he needed to gather strong grass to make unbreakable ties and then weave strand after strand.

Every time with each aircraft taking off, a dream was planted in his mind to fly in an aeroplane. He would be the first from his village to fly in an aircraft. It reminded him of his village. In his imagination, he saw his mother sending him to the kitchen garden by the river to get vegetables, but he did not return. Instead, he kept walking along the river till he reached the old orchard. A view of a large meadow, a pond with floating lotus flowers, a herd of cattle and another village on the further bank and a temple on a higher ground that reflected the setting sun suddenly opened before him. He walked along the mud houses and his mother questioned him about the vegetables when he reached home. He saw his mother yelling and running after him with a stick and he ran out of the house to get the vegetables.

The sun hid behind the hill, the air began to lose its dryness and lucidity and the little bird was lost in the increasing darkness. The profound stillness was broken from time to time by a roaring jet engine and a long beam of light flashing on the runway. Anubhav came out of the world of his dreams, jumped off the wall and started pacing along the road again.

5

SUCCESS LIES INSIDE A LABYRINTH

For months, Anubhav was idle for six days a week. Then, on Wednesday, he would pore over the newspaper editorial with a handful of job postings. He emailed in response to over a hundred job postings but had yet to get a single response. The Times Ascent was light enough to see a long way down the abandoned street and seemed more like dawn or dusk rather than night, but was not enough to dispel the darkness. He needed to reach out to a company.

It was another Wednesday and the paper cuttings from the Times Ascent were ready for another week's venture. Anubhav was having breakfast with the newspaper in his hand. He looked over the astrology section of the newspaper. It stated:

'Horoscope today, astrological prediction for Cancer: Today, you are blessed with a positive moon, you may feel good and maybe more creative and you may recognize the value of intellectual assets. You may meet with some influential person who may help you get benefits. You can start some new investments with the help of your siblings or any other network, which may be helpful in the growth of a business. It is recommended to take proper rest to maintain your enthusiasm.'

This quick glimpse enormously influenced his imagination. He was thinking precisely along the same lines.

"The stars too are supportive of doing something new," the swallowed words had not pronounced them as written.

Anubhav firmly believed in astrology and the science of stars and that the position of the planets and stars influences human life. In his view of life, everything that happens to us, even the smallest or seemingly most insignificant event, happens for some particular reason, and stars prepare the ground for it.

Whenever he read a newspaper, he craved to know what was written in the daily horoscope section. His sun sign was Cancer with ascendant Libra, so he would read the predictions of both. Indeed, the intensity of his work for the next six days after the excursion was ruled by what had been predicted.

Breakfast was over and it was time to connect with the recruiters. He had located a telephone booth in the cantonment market outside the hospital, but there was an opportunity to make free calls from the hospital ward.

As usual, he went to the hospital ward to see his uncle and to call the telephone numbers he had marked in the newspaper cuttings. His uncle had been in charge of a patient ward recently and it had become easy for him to call from this ward. It was a ward where patients with long-term ailments were admitted and there were hardly any severe cases. Most patients were healthy enough to do routine work, roam around and care for themselves.

The doctor used to visit the patients once a day and the rest of the time, his uncle was the only person monitoring the patients. The phone remained unoccupied most of the time. The staff room had a computer, and a printer attached to it. It was not connected to the internet, but was still helpful. He could take any number of printouts, free of cost.

The computers were new in most of the hospital departments. This new machine allowed Anubhav to impress the staff by training them in the operation of the computer and its basics. The entire nursing staff had become known to him and they used to call him if there was an issue with their computer, most of the time to learn about a feature they did not know.

Since he visited frequently, he became attached to the ward's patients and mingled with them. Occasionally, he would spend entire days talking to them and watching TV or live games there.

That day, he had a couple of phone numbers to call. These phone numbers were in a small advertisement box in the newspaper every week, but no job details were shared except stating that all graduates were eligible, including freshers. These phone numbers belonged to placement consultancies. He wanted to get information about them.

Since there was nobody in the staff room, he dialed the number in the newspaper cutting.

The phone rang, and a lady answered, "Hello, Career Point. This is Varsha speaking."

"Hello, madam. My name is Anubhav Gumrah," said Anubhav over the phone in a muffled voice. "I am a graduate in computer engineering and I am looking for a placement."

"Welcome, Anubhav. We specialize in providing recruitment services," returned the lady at the other end and asked, "May I know what your qualifications are and if you are experienced or a fresher?"

"I am a graduate in computer engineering. I graduated this year and I am a fresher. Do you have any requirements?"

"Yes, we have several clients looking for freshers..."

Anubhav interrupted, "Which company?"

"You must visit us first and then we will inform you about the job opportunities and share the details of the clients," she explained further and added, "There is a one-time registration fee of five hundred rupees."

"A fee! Ok, how can I reach there?"

"We are located in Ashok Vijay Complex, MG Road in Camp. We are open between 10:00 a.m. and 5:00 p.m."

"Thank you, madam. I will be there tomorrow," said Anubhav and put down the phone. Someone was walking into the staff room.

Anubhav was delighted at the thought of facing an interview through a placement consultancy, but had one concern. He was still to determine how much money he had left and was uncertain if he had enough money to pay the registration charges.

The sound of someone walking could be heard outside the staff room door.

"Anubhav, the movie has begun and your friends are calling you," said his uncle, entering the room.

Anubhav, who was sitting in his uncle's chair, stood up and went to the TV room.

A patient pushed a chair towards him while others made room for him to sit. A new movie was being shown for the first time on television. However, he was worried about the amount of money left with him.

"Excuse me," he said in a sad voice. "I have to go somewhere else."

He decided to go back home and quickly reached the quarter. He first wanted to count the money he had left and rushed to open his briefcase. He kept all his money in its side pocket.

"One hundred, two hundred, three hundred... eleven hundred," he counted. There were eleven hundred rupees in it.

It was the last week of the month and he was about to receive the monthly tuition payments soon. In addition to this, there was enough money in his wallet to travel to the city a couple more times. The tension that had etched lines upon his countenance vanished as he found sufficient money to register with the placement consultancy.

It was about nine o'clock in the morning on the following day when he walked to the Goliber Maidan bus stop. As he passed by the newspaper vendor there, he waved his hand at him.

"Hello, sir. How are you today?" asked the vendor.

"I am doing fine, thanks," he said and further questioned, "Do you know where the Ashok Vijay Complex is located?"

The newspaper vendor smiled as if he had been waiting for Anubhav to ask him for the directions to a new location. Mustafa had become his guide and every time Anubhav had to visit a new place, he inquired about its location from him before boarding a bus.

"It's near the Camp bus stand, about a quarter of a mile, once you get down from the bus there," answered the vendor.

The sun was rising and offices and shops were opening their shutters. Anubhav realized that the consultancy was nearby and he could easily reach there on foot. Thanking the newspaper vendor, he started walking in the direction of the Camp bus stop, thinking that it would kill some time and save the fare.

He walked through the Camp market. It was one of the most vibrant places in the city and was getting ready for the day. The shops on the streets, malls and numerous food stalls were opening their shutters and people had started gathering. The breeze, which had been cool when he had left the quarter, turned warmer and the roar of the increasing traffic took over. Strolling through the market alongside the MG Road and reading the names of each shop, he finally arrived at the Ashok Vijay Complex.

A security guard was sitting at the gate on a stool. Although he was not questioning anyone, he was looking at everyone intently, much like a detective. Everyone was walking around freely inside the building and

Anubhav followed the others to reach the lobby where the elevators were located.

Many offices were in the same building and their names and respective floor numbers were marked on a board that was displayed in the lobby. He looked at the centre of the board where it was written '206: Career Point.' Seeing this, he was assured that he was at the right place. He took the lift to the second floor to the office of Carrier Point consultancy.

It was a 20x15 square feet room with a couple of partitioned glass cubicles at one side that were visible from the door outside the gate. Just upon entering the office, there was a reception desk. A statue of Lord Ganesha was placed at one corner of the table, with a garland of fresh flowers. There were benches and chairs opposite to it and a few candidates were sitting in them with their heads lowered, as they were writing something. He walked to the reception counter and approached the lady sitting there. "Good morning, madam," greeted the young man. "I am here to meet Ms. Varsha. Are you her?"

The receptionist was a fifty-year-old lady, but the voice on the phone had sounded much younger when he had spoken to her the previous day.

"Good morning, sir," she acknowledged. "No, I am Monika. Varsha will be coming late today. Could you please tell me what you need from her?"

"I talked to her yesterday about the job opening for freshers."

"I can help you with that. May I have your resume?"

"Here it is. May I know for which company you are hiring?" inquired Anubhav, handing over his resume to her.

"Hexaware Technology. You need to complete the registration formalities and then I will share more details," she mentioned, looking at his resume.

Monika explained the procedure. Anubhav needed to pay upfront a one-time registration charge of five hundred rupees. She promised that their consultancy would share his resume with recruiters and market it for various job positions. After his profile was shortlisted, he would need to go through the company's interview process. Once selected, one month's salary was required to be paid to the consultancy for their services.

It seemed to be an attractive deal and Anubhav liked the idea. There were promising job opportunities and he would be required to pay one month's salary only after getting a job. It was a lucrative proposal, and he accepted the terms without a second thought.

"Sure, madam. I agree to your terms."

"In addition to this, if you have any friends and you bring them to us, you will get referral money," the lady added.

"When is the interview for Hexaware Technology? Where is the office located and when do I need to go there?" Anubhav queried at once.

"The interview is going on. There is a qualifying round," explained Monika. "I will give you the question paper and you will be required to take a written test. Once you clear the screening test, the company will call you for the next round."

"In which programming language would you like to take the test?" she questioned further.

It was weird that there was no company representative present and the test could be taken as per his choice, but there was no reason to be suspicious of anything she had mentioned.

He thought for a while and answered, "C and C++."

This was the programming language that he had learned the most and prepared in college.

"Ok, fill this form first," instructed Monika, handing over the application form to him.

"You can take a seat there and fill it carefully. Meanwhile, I will organize the test for you."

He sat at a table in another corner and then, looked at the form carefully. It was the first time he was filling out an employment form. He read each section from top to bottom and then, from bottom to top. He filled it out carefully and revised it twice. When he was satisfied, he went back to the receptionist.

"Here it is, madam," he said, looking at her directly.

Monika accepted the form, wrote a number on it for the record and tore off its lower portion.

"These are your registration details and receipt," she said, giving the lower portion of the form back to him. "Keep it safe with you."

"Five hundred rupees, please," she said, requesting the registration charge. Anubhav gave her a five hundred rupee note and his registration was completed.

The question paper was ready. It consisted of fifty questions that were a mix of easy to medium complexity level in C and C++.

He couldn't complete the paper in thirty minutes and the time was over. He was about to stand up from his seat and give it back but noticed that the other candidates who had reached before him were still writing the test, with their heads lowered. He had almost stood up, but looking at the others, he remained seated and concentrated once again on completing the test. Monika was busy dealing with newcomers and paid no attention to them. Although it was a thirty-minute test, the candidates took their time to return the answer sheet.

Anubhav took advantage of the leniency and moved only when he finished the test. He revised it twice and returned the answer sheet when he was satisfied with the answers.

"Give me a call after two days," said Monika. "I will let you know if you have qualified for the next round." One round of the recruitment process had been completed, and he was free to go.

What kind of test was this? It was open to everybody at any time, with no time limit. Everyone took as much time as they wanted. Is this the way recruitment is carried out in a company?

He came outside the office and walked towards the gallery where many other applicants stood, speaking to each other. He was excited to find someone in the same boat and wanted to know how others were exploring job opportunities. He talked to some job seekers who had also attempted the same test.

"This is a fabricated test," said someone in the group, in a discouraged voice. "There is no recruitment going on in Hexaware Technology. I have been to their office. This job consultancy is fraudulent and cheating us."

Anubhav ignored him, thinking why would someone take out an advertisement in a newspaper? The service fee had to be paid only after getting an offer letter. Anubhav didn't find any basis to believe him and neither did the others.

While roaming around the marketplace which had now become lively, he found the sign board of another job consultancy by the name of Career Builder, in the adjacent building. He was eager to visit it and stepped into the office without losing any time.

There was a similar set up with the same course of action. After getting the offer letter, the candidates needed to pay one month's salary towards the services, but a one-time registration charge of five hundred rupees was required to be paid upfront.

Anubhav was trapped. More consultancies meant more interview opportunities. He wanted to register here as well but was in a dilemma. He had only six hundred rupees left for the remainder of the month.

He needed to wait for at least one or two weeks to get the tuition payments from his pupils. He left, promising to revisit the office the following week.

If you find the right path, success is quite close. This thought kindled the lamp of hope in him. He could relate to astrology more closely after finding the placement consultancy, which made him feel festive. Throughout the journey back home, he was pondering over every detail of the question paper and whether he had answered correctly or not, but he had to wait for two more days for the results.

The following two days were longer than usual. Waiting for the result of an examination is more fearful than the exam itself. Anubhav was very nervous and visited the temple twice a day and prayed to qualify for the next round.

At last, the moment arrived. Two days later, the clock struck ten, and it was time for the Carrier Point placement consultancy office to open.

He was excited to call Monika. Using the hospital phone in his uncle's ward in the morning hours was difficult as it was the time for the doctor's rounds. He would have had to wait longer if he had gone there. So, he went to the public telephone booth in Mira market outside the hospital campus.

He dialed the number, and the phone rang. "Hello, Career Point," answered a lady on the other side.

"Can I speak to Monika, please?" he asked in an impatient voice.

"Yes, this is Monika here. Who is this speaking?"

"Good morning, madam. This is Anubhav. I took the written test two days ago, and you had instructed me to call today."

"You have not been selected," she promptly replied, without sparing a single second.

His heart broke and skipped a beat. After a pause, he asked, "May I know what the cut-off mark is?"

"Sorry, we don't disclose this," the lady stated. "It is against the company's policy."

Anubhav was shaken, but he didn't question the integrity of the consultancy. He asked if there was any other opportunity with any other company but she replied that he needed to wait for it. "We will inform you once we get a new job opening suitable for you," she promised.

Anubhav returned with a gloomy face but the prompt response that she had given him stating that he had not qualified, raised suspicion in his mind. She should have responded by asking him about the company or position for which he had applied. Many candidates had applied for different job profiles in the company.

"It should take at least ten seconds to check a result and go through a list," he thought. "Perhaps that fellow had been right that it was a fabricated test."

Anyway, he wanted to move on and had discovered more placement consultancies as well and had talked to them over the phone. One job consultancy that he found was named Pathfinder. The registration fee was only two hundred rupees. His earnings from giving tuitions to children were limited and he could only register for a couple more placement consultancies the following month.

Anubhav waited impatiently for the first week of the following month. When he received enough money from his students for tuitions, he decided to visit Career Builder, the second placement consultancy and the third, Pathfinder, which he had shortlisted.

In Career Builder, he found that the process was similar in every manner as before, including registration and a written test. Though the exam pattern was similar, the name of the company was different. He completed all the formalities and attempted the written test. Like in the first consultancy, he was asked to call back after two days. He was sure that he had done better and would qualify for the next round this time.

The third consultancy, Pathfinder, was located on Dhole Patil Road and he boarded a bus to reach there.

Unlike the other two, this consultancy had an office in a two-storey residential building. This place was not deserted but not lively either and there was hardly any bustle. A sign board with the name of the consultancy inscribed on it was hung outside an apartment on the ground floor of the building. The building was also old-style and different from the shining offices of the first two consultancies he had visited.

"This consultancy is not getting business," he muttered, looking at the dilapidated buildings on the empty street.

The door was open and as he entered it, he saw an office boy standing on a chair and organizing the files in a rusted and stained cupboard. It looked as though the files had been in the cupboard for years. The racks were partitioned year-wise and arranged in increasing order from bottom to top. There were many red binders marked with the year of the date. It was an old-fashioned office. Folders marked with years of the 1990s were also arranged in the other cupboard. He assumed that these held the profiles and applications of the candidates who had registered there.

"Hi, I have come here for the registration," Anubhav said politely.

The office boy stepped down from the chair.

"Sandeep sir has gone home for lunch," he said. "He will come back soon. Please have a seat."

"Will it take time?"

"He should come downstairs soon."

The consultant's apartment was above his office and he ran this consultancy from a residential building.

There were no other candidates, which strengthened Anubhav's doubt whether he was at the right place or not.

It took about an hour for the owner of the office to return. His name was Sandeep Bhosley. He was a short, modest man with grey hair and was around fifty years old. When he entered the office, the office boy notified him, "Sir, a candidate is waiting for you."

Anubhav stood up and looked at him, "Good afternoon, sir. My name is Anubhav."

"Good afternoon. Have you been here before? I don't remember you."

"No, sir. I am coming here for the first time. We spoke over the phone last week."

"Oh yes, now I remember your name. Are you a graduate in computer engineering?" He asked. "Do I remember correctly?"

"Yes, sir, you are right."

"Excellent!" said Sandeep. He stated further, "Disha Technology is looking for fresh computer science graduates."

"Yes, sure," nodded Anubhav, anticipating a similar procedure this time. "Is the qualifying test going to be held today itself?"

"No, it needs to be scheduled. I will share your profile with the company's HR and they will call if you are shortlisted," Sandeep explained to him.

Anubhav became alert as he had had different experiences with the other two consultancies. He was confused about whether to register here and spend more money, since he suspected something fishy in these job consultancies. However, this looked more promising than the other two and the company's HR was involved in the selection process here. The first two consultancies had evaded his questions about sharing any information about the companies, except for their names. However, there was only one way to confirm if this consultancy was fishy or not. He had to pay for it if he wanted to know the truth.

Truth reveals itself but he had not known that it would require a payment. He decided to register to find out the truth, if not a job.

He completed the registration formalities. Sandeep made a photocopy of Anubhav's resume and put a stamp on it, bearing the name and address of his consultancy. He signed on top of the seal on the resume and handing it over to him said, "Give me a call next Monday. I should get the details of the shortlisted candidates by then."

The day's schedule was completed, and he was returning to the quarter, but a riddle had been sparked in his mind. All three consultancies had similar methods of making money by taking one month's salary if a candidate was selected, but different methods of operation. The first two consultancies had no job requirements and took a fraudulent examination to attract candidates and raise money, by charging a registration fee. Why did they refuse to share more information about the relevant company, location, and HR? Sandeep didn't hold any such test and was transparent about sharing the details of the job and company profile.

Charging more money for enrollment alone should not cause the questioning of one's integrity. The fellow in the group who had called it a fraudulent consultancy on the first day of registration with Career Point may have had a point, but nobody paid attention to it.

He relaxed his mind and decided to wait for the result of the test he had taken in Career Builder, before coming to any conclusion. Anubhav wanted to find out the truth, so he planned to play a trick this time.

Two days passed, and he called the Career Builder office.

A lady answered the call and said, "Good morning, Career Builder."

"Hello, madam. Good morning. I am Rajesh," he said. He didn't reveal his actual name and pretended to be someone else. "I had taken the written test two days back, and you had asked me to call today."

"You are not selected," answered the lady spontaneously, without a thought.

It was the same pattern.

"Madam, it seems like you have not checked the list. Can you please check it once more?" He wanted the lady to verify it.

"I have checked it," she maintained, without hesitation. "Your name is not on the list of selected candidates."

"May I know the cut-off? I have cross-verified all the questions and answers and I am certain that my score will be more than ninety percent," said Anubhav, who was not ready to accept her reply. "Can you please share my scorecard with me?"

"I am sorry, we can't disclose it," insisted the lady, unwilling to give any information. "This is against the policy of the company."

"I understand your policy. You don't have any business apart from cheating unemployed youths and charging five hundred rupees just for registration," retorted Anubhav and there was anger in his voice this time. "You are using the name of a big company to lure job seekers. Otherwise, you would have taken a few minutes to check the result and verify candidate details before giving an answer so promptly."

The lady at the opposite end was stunned and remained silent for thirty seconds. Then, she yelled loudly, "How can you say this?"

"I can say this because I am not Rajesh. My name is Anubhav," he said in a normal voice this time. "Now, please check your selection list if Anubhav Gumrah has been selected or not?"

The lady disconnected the call instantly. She had been caught red-handed and Anubhav had been successful in trapping her. The truth had been revealed.

There were thousands of candidates graduating every year. A small advertisement in a leading newspaper was sufficient to prey on these youths. Receiving even a registration fee would rake in a good amount of money every month.

He was convinced that the first two consultancies were fraudulent and fabricating a written test to fool candidates. Everyone was eligible for it: a fresher, an experienced person or even one without a degree.

Anubhav had been deceived and cheated by fraudulent job consultants but it taught him a lesson that success lies within a chakravyuh (labyrinth).

The chakravyuh in *The Mahabharata* was a formation of many soldiers standing together in a spiral shape, which became harder to conquer as a person reached the inner layers. Not every warrior could destroy it.

Extraordinary skills were required to break through a chakravyuh. Abhimanyu was in his mother, Subhadra's womb, when Arjuna narrated the technique of chakravyuh and how the numerous circles could be penetrated to her.

When the war between the Kauravas and the Pandavas took place, Abhimanyu decided to enter the chakravyuh to save the honour of the Pandavas. Nobody could help him in the middle of the battle at that time and he could not escape it.

Like Abhimanyu, Anubhav had learned that there were many IT companies in Pune but didn't know what would come next. There was nobody to guide him and show him the right path.

What appears to be isn't always the truth and what is true isn't always visible clearly. There are friends and foes everywhere that form the circles of a chakravyuh. Success lies inside this chakravyuh. Abhimanyu had entered it and didn't come out of it but Anubhav couldn't be a martyr. He had to discover a way to get out of it. If he had to save his family's honour, he had to enter the chakravyuh and break every circle.

6

THE FIRST PUNCH OF ACHIEVEMENT

It was a Sunday evening and though the sun was yet to set, the heat of the day was diminishing steadily. Sunday was a holiday for Anubhav's uncle and they were sitting at a small table on the verandah, having tea with cutlets. Anubhav was silently looking at the children playing in the playground on the opposite side of the road, lost in thought. The flies and mosquitoes were buzzing persistently, and it was pleasant to reflect that it would soon be nightfall. His uncle stood up from the chair, closed the door and window screen and moved towards him.

"How is your job search going on?" asked his uncle, breaking the silence. "Nowadays, you have stopped coming to the hospital and your aunt informed me that you remain outside for most part of the day."

Anubhav came out of his daydream and shared the week's experience with him about the three placement consultancies he had visited.

"Sandeep seems trustworthy," said Anubhav optimistically. "This week, I should get an interview call if his consultancy is carrying out its business honestly."

"Don't give a single penny to anyone. They will do it without money if they have any job requirements," advised his uncle. "You should be careful of job fraud and scams."

"Yes, I understand it now," he replied doubtfully. "I will go to the Pathfinder office again to try to find out more details to figure out if anything is wrong."

"You should file a police complaint against the first two cheaters," his uncle suggested. "I will come with you to the police station."

Anubhav disagreed with his uncle as he intended to get a job and not waste time on others' misdoings. Sandeep had asked Anubhav to call him by Monday to check whether his profile had been shortlisted by Disha Technology. Anubhav was curious to know about it but at the same time, he was skeptical. So, he decided to visit his office and meet him personally.

He revisited Sandeep's office the next day. The sun was about to ascend above the head. It was the same old building in the Kothrud area. Like his previous visit, not many job aspirants were present, but a girl could be seen sitting in a chair across the room, reading a magazine with her head lowered, her loose hair covering her face. Sandeep had just ended a conversation with someone over the phone.

"Good morning, sir," he greeted Sandeep as he entered the office.

"Come in, Anubhav. Good morning. You have come at the right moment. I was talking to the HR of Disha Technologies. Yours and Ridima's profiles have been shortlisted for the position of software engineer," said Sandeep, with a satisfied smile, looking first at him and then at the girl who was busy reading a journal. Anubhav didn't need to guess who Ridima was.

The moment Sandeep spoke, she lifted her face, holding her hair back and looked at him with a bright smile. The next moment, she turned towards Anubhav and looked at him but her smile faded.

However, Anubhav caught a flash of her face for the first time. Two black dazzling eyes held him fast like magnets. He couldn't see anything else at that moment and kept looking at her until she averted her eyes from him and turned her face down again. She put the magazine back on the side table.

"Do you have a passport-size photograph?" Sandeep asked both of them simultaneously.

"Yes, sir, I have it," replied Anubhav, taking out a photograph from a folder in his backpack.

Ridima also looked in her handbag and approached Sandeep's table to give him the photograph. Sandeep took out copies of their resumes from his file and glued their respective photos onto the top right corner. Then he put a stamp and signed on them.

"Both of you need to go to Disha Technology's office on Friday," he said, handing over their resumes to them. "It is located in Aundh. Give this to Bruno."

"Thank you, sir," Anubhav was prompt to respond.

"Best of luck to both of you," said Sandeep. "Do not forget to give me a call after the test."

An interview date was fixed and Anubhav was glad that he was finally at the right place after falling into the hands of two deceitful consultancies. Ridima left the room, with her resume in her hand but Anubhav remained there as he was inquisitive.

"Sir, may I ask you a question?"

"Sure."

"I regularly look at newspapers and job postings but I never see such a job opening for young graduates."

Sandeep informed him that Pathfinder was their recruitment partner. Disha Technology was his direct client, and the recruiters used to share their job requirements with him. Generally, if the openings were small in number, the company preferred local candidates and didn't post this in any public forum.

Anubhav understood why he had not been able to attend any interviews so far. He was convinced with Sandeep's answer and left. He needed to go to the bus stop that was about a mile from the office.

He had just walked around a hundred metres when he found Ridima standing near the road junction, next to Sandeep's office. He could easily recognize her from a distance. It looked like she was waiting for someone. As he moved closer, he could see her completely for the first time.

Anubhav's face beamed as he looked at her. She was a thin, petite girl of around twenty-two, slim, with a round, fair face and black hair. Her nose was long and sharp and her chin, too, was rounded. Her eyelashes were long, the corners of her mouth were sharp and due to this general sharpness, the expression on her face was extremely stern.

She wore a mint and cream salwar suit, painted with leaves in shades of lime green with embroidered sides and had wrapped a white cotton scarf around her neck. Her appearance was more radiant than the lustre of her apparel, flawless and prettier, with sharp elbows and long pink fingers. She reminded him of a portrait of a medieval princess.

She stood straight, looking at the road and didn't turn to look at him. When an auto-rickshaw passed by her, she raised her hand towards it, signalling it to stop. She turned her scarf towards the back using her right hand, leaned forward and got into it. She asked the driver to go some place. Anubhav could hear her musical voice but couldn't listen to precisely what she said. Anubhav had slowed his pace to almost zero. Then, the auto left that place and he started walking again.

Anubhav resumed walking towards the bus stand, but his mind remained behind at the junction he had just now crossed. He couldn't remember seeing such a beautiful girl before. It was not Wednesday today, the only day he used to buy a newspaper but now, he desired to know the astrology predictions. 'I should certainly buy today's newspaper and read the astrology section. There must be something miraculous in it,' he thought and reached the bus stop.

Unfortunately, his favourite newspaper vendor had closed the shop and left for the day when Anubhav reached there, so he was deprived of reading the astrology prediction for the day.

He reached home and by evening, he had made up his mind. He should forget about the most beautiful face he had ever seen and focus on studying. The joy of receiving the first opportunity for an interview triumphed over the feeling of seeing Ridima, when he arrived at the quarter. Friday was close and only four days remained. He didn't want to miss this opportunity, so he prepared a plan and started working on it the same day.

A four-day wait was short and soon, it was Friday. Anubhav was ready to face the test. He got ready and double-checked the documents in his folder. He took out the resume that Sandeep had given him and checked it twice to ensure that he was carrying the magic ticket to meet a recruiter.

Like other days, he walked to the Goliber Maidan bus stop. He has memorized all the bus numbers and routes by now and he didn't need to ask the newspaper vendor for directions. However, the courtesy smile and hand waving continued as before. He caught a bus for IT Park at Aundh-Hinjewadi Link Road.

He got down at a bus stop in front of the Disha Technology office. Two security guards were standing outside the building and people were coming in and going out without being questioned. He followed them but one of the security guards stopped him as he approached the gate.

"Sir, please show me your identity card."

Anubhav noticed that all the others were the company's employees and wore a card hanging with a ribbon around their neck.

"I am here for the interview," he said, opening the folder in his hand and took out the resume that Sandeep had attested.

"Which HR do you need to meet?" questioned the security guard. "Do you have a phone number or extension?"

"Bruno... but I don't know his number."

The guard quickly looked through the directory with him and dialed somebody. After a short conversation, he passed Anubhav a visitor register and asked him to enter his details in it. The guard then handed him a visitor's pass and clipped it on top of the pocket of his shirt. By this time, Anubhav had become acquainted with the security practices of an IT company.

"Go to the second floor," said the guard and directed him to the path towards the lift in the building.

Anubhav took the lift and reached the second floor. As he came out of it, he looked at the lobby next to the gallery. There was a glass door and a big, shining nameplate with 'Disha Technology, Development Center' written in big letters. He was excited that he was at the right place and his doubts about Sandeep's consultancy were dispelled. He wiped his perspiring face and arranged the crease of his shirt and trousers before moving ahead.

Anubhav took out the resume from his backpack and moved towards the reception. Two young ladies were sitting and continuously talking over the phone. It was a quarter to eleven on his watch but the three wall clocks hanging opposite the welcome desk, displayed different times. The countries' names were written below the clocks: India, Australia and the USA. He could easily guess it was a multinational company, and the clocks were there to show the time in the different time zones where the company was operating.

"Good morning, madam," he said, handing over the copy of his resume to one of the ladies. "I am here for an interview."

The receptionist looked at it and noticed the stamp on the resume.

"Have you come through Pathfinder?" she asked.

"Yes, madam."

"Have a seat there. I will inform Bruno," she said, returning the resume and directed him to a nearby waiting area in the lobby.

Anubhav walked towards the lobby. The reception waiting area was about twenty steps to the left, where several sofas and couches were arranged. As he approached them, he almost stopped breathing and his eyes opened wide. Ridima was sitting on a two-seater sofa. He knew that she was supposed to attend the interview but didn't know when she would be coming and hadn't considered seeing her again. Both of them looked at each other. She was dressed in gray business formal trousers and a pleated-neck printed top. Her coal-black hair was tied in a single braid that hung down to her waist. She looked very different from when he had first seen her; a perfect executive.

"Hi," said Ridima, with a beaming smile.

He was not expecting her to give him such a warm response.

"Hi. You are Ridima, right?"

"Yes…" she said, pausing as though she had forgotten his name.

"My name is Anubhav."

"Yes, I remember it," Ridima broke her reserve with a giggle. "Sandeep mentioned it that day."

Her friendly behaviour evoked a dazed smile from Anubhav. He couldn't have even dreamt that she would ever speak to him.

"Yes, you are right," said Anubhav. "I thought you didn't notice me that day," he said. "By the way, did you find Bruno?"

"No. I have been waiting for half an hour, but nobody has appeared."

"Oh, I was worried that I would be late."

The recruiter was busy with his work, which allowed them to get to know each other. Ridima had completed her engineering at a college in Bhopal that year like Anubhav. Her father was an engineer in Bharat Heavy Electricals Ltd. and she had been brought up in Bhopal.

They talked to each other and everyone passing the waiting area looked at her.

'She has a million-dollar face value; she will be selected for sure,' Anubhav weighed in his mind.

After an hour passed, an HR representative approached them and said, "Ridima and Anubhav?"

"Yes, sir," they both responded together and stood up from the sofa.

"I am Bruno," the recruiter introduced himself.

Bruno was a tall, clean-shaven young boy, who looked a little older than Anubhav. He asked for their resumes and looked at them.

"Did Sandeep inform you about the interview process?" he questioned further.

"Yes, but not in much detail," replied Ridima.

"Ok, there is going to be an online test first," Bruno clarified. "Then, an HR interview will follow a technical round, if you qualify it," he continued, while leading them to another area. "Please follow me."

He brought them to a big hall where there were many cubicles that had desktops in each corner; some occupied and some free. Bruno used to sit in one corner of the hall. He took them to his desk and logged on to his desktop. Then, he wrote something on two Post-its.

"This is your username and password," he explained, giving one to each of them. "You can use any desktop that is free. Go through the instructions carefully before you start the test. You can take your time to read the instructions before you begin, but the timer will start once you click the 'Start the Test' button."

They both occupied a cubicle each and became engrossed in the test. It was an hour-long test with two sections. The first section covered programming, database and computer knowledge, while the second was an aptitude test.

Anubhav completed it first and turning to Bruno's desk said, "Sir, I have finished the test."

"Excellent, you are done for the day," said the recruiter and further added, "I will share the result with Sandeep by next week."

Anubhav thanked him and left the room, glancing at where Ridima was sitting. She had also finished and while he was leaving the room, he saw her going towards Bruno.

Anubhav anticipated that Ridima would come outside the room, so he remained in the waiting area where they had been sitting. She also came out in less than five minutes.

Both came out of the office building. There were auto-rickshaws standing in a queue alongside the road, waiting for customers. Ridima walked towards them and Anubhav accompanied her.

Ridima stopped suddenly, skimmed her bag and took out her cell phone. She dialled a number and began talking to somebody. It was a Nokia 6600, the latest model of Nokia that had been newly released. Anubhav looked at it curiously.

Sandeep was on the line. She informed him about the test and then, handing over her mobile phone to Anubhav asked him, "Do you want to speak to Sandeep?"

"Sure, thank you so much."

Anubhav told Sandeep that he had done well in the programming part but couldn't complete the second section on aptitude and general reasoning and had finished only half of it. More time was required to complete all the questions as the problems were complex.

"Don't worry. You do not need to score a hundred percent," Sandeep reassured him on the phone. "I will connect with Bruno and call you once I come to know about the result."

The call was disconnected. Anubhav thanked Ridima, returning the phone to her.

"I need to go to Kothrud." She inquired, "Where do you stay?"

Ridima stayed with a few friends in a rented apartment in the Kothrud area.

"I stay in the cantonment area, next to Kothrud," he answered.

"Oh, it's the same way," she said, offering to share the ride. "You can come with me."

Anubhav had only taken an auto-rickshaw when he had come to Pune for the first time and always travelled by the city buses, which were much cheaper. He thought this would give him extra time to talk with her, but he controlled his emotions and considered how much money was there in his wallet. He had already taken a favour from her by using her cell phone, so the ride would be on him.

"Thank you," he said, making an excuse. "I need to go somewhere else today. Please carry on."

"Ok, I should leave then."

She entered the auto-rickshaw standing there and then, waved her hand, bidding him farewell with a smile. Anubhav waited for the auto-rickshaw to leave the place. After it had left, he started walking towards the bus stop, looking for a bus on route number 177 towards the MG Road bus stop. There was no direct bus to Goliber Maidan from that place.

Ridima might think about him after the test and he wished to meet her too. However, he did not think about talking with her. Not only had he seen her again, but also, had spoken to her for an hour.

He was not thinking about Ridima, unlike the first time he had seen her; instead, the question paper that he had attempted was of more interest at this time. He was constantly going over it in his mind and trying to recall what he had answered. He was confident that the programming and database section had gone well but he hadn't been able to complete many questions in the reasoning and analytical part. He was worried that this could impact his chances of qualifying for the first round. He kept praying to god to give him this opportunity all the way back to the quarter.

Anubhav kept calling Sandeep every day, but Bruno shared no update. So, when a week had passed, he went and saw him in person.

"Congratulations, Anubhav. You have qualified for the next round," Sandeep informed him as he entered the office. Anubhav was overjoyed on hearing this and asked, "What about the girl who was there with me, Ridima?"

"She has not qualified. I have sent ten candidates there so far, but no one could clear the first round," revealed Sandeep. "You are the first one to clear it from my consultancy."

Anubhav was thrilled but at the same time, disheartened on hearing that Ridima didn't make it. Though he had enjoyed her company only for an hour, he couldn't forget her easily.

Sandeep asked him if he could attend the next interview round the following day. Anubhav had waited for this opportunity for months and conveyed his readiness promptly. He didn't have the patience to wait any longer.

It was all happening so fast that Anubhav couldn't believe it, but he felt happy. He had struggled for months to knock on the right door and had learnt how the outcome changed when one worked with the right people at the right place.

Reaching the office of Disha Technology the next day was easy as he had been there the previous week. He took a seat in the waiting area, waiting for the recruiter. Six more candidates were waiting for the interview along with him, sitting silently and not even looking at each other. He remembered Ridima and thought she would have made a difference. The atmosphere would not have been so dull and silent if she had been there.

An unfamiliar HR representative called the candidates one by one. It took the entire day for him to finish the interview. First, there were two rounds of technical interviews, followed by an HR interview. Finally, Bruno called him. He completed some formalities, asking Anubhav about his salary expectation and explaining the company benefits and policies. At last, he told him he could leave and instructed him to follow up with Sandeep to know the final result. Bruno was not supposed to share the interview results directly with the candidates if they belonged to a placement consultancy.

Everything went well. Considering Bruno's body language and how he had explained the company policies and benefits, Anubhav was hopeful that the interview had gone well. He was expecting the offer letter.

A week had passed since the final interview with Disha Technology had been completed. Anubhav was getting more and more excited with each passing day but wanted to avoid showing his restlessness by following up with Sandeep.

On the evening of the seventh day, his uncle returned from duty and asked if he had shared the hospital's number with anyone.

"Yes, I have shared it," said Anubhav reluctantly. "Was there a call for me?"

"Someone named Sandeep had called and asked for you," informed his uncle, sharing a phone number. "He requested you to call him on this number."

Since Anubhav didn't have a cell phone and nor did his uncle have a telephone at his residence, he used to share the phone number of his uncle's ward in his contact details. It was Sandeep's phone number and hence, must be related to the interview. Anubhav could guess this quickly and looked at the clock on the wall; the hour hand had passed seven. Sandeep's office would be closed. He would have to wait till the next morning.

He drifted off into a restless sleep, praying for a positive result. The following day, he woke up early; the sun had yet to rise and when he looked outside the window, it was still dark. He strolled in and out of the house restlessly, sometimes on the front lawn and at other times, in the backyard and then went for a long walk, listening to the singing and chirping of the birds. The first rays of sunlight touched the ground and the early morning chorus of melodic birdsong drifted in. But it didn't attract him as he was waiting for the clock to strike ten, when Sandeep would be in the office.

As the clock's hand touched ten, he raced to the nearest public telephone booth in the market outside the hospital campus and dialled Sandeep.

"Good morning, sir. This is Anubhav here."

"Hi, Anubhav. Good morning. I was trying to reach you," said Sandeep. "I left a message for you on the number you shared."

"Yes sir, that number belongs to my uncle's workplace." Anubhav took a deep breath and said, "I don't have a mobile."

"No problem. I have good news for you," declared Sandeep. "You have been selected by Disha Technology for the post of Trainee Software Engineer."

At first, Anubhav couldn't believe it, but there was an explosion of joy within him. A symphony of jubilation erupted as he heard the news and he could not utter a word.

"Thank you, sir," he replied, controlling his feelings. He added, "I will see you tomorrow," and put down the receiver. He wanted to see him personally and thank him.

A storm of feelings, thoughts and memories suddenly arose within him and he could not breathe properly nor remain in the same place. He hastened to the counter to pay the telephone operator and walked out rapidly, without collecting the change. Joy erupted within him, gladdening his heart and he longed to breathe, run and live!

He had been selected for a company and wanted to share his happiness with someone. He felt as though he had wings and ran madly towards the hospital ward, not looking at anything on the way. His feet hardly touched the ground and he could have hit a bike, a moving car or an auto-rickshaw on the road or even a tree standing near the road. His mind didn't register anything around, and he gazed at the blue sky. He was in the seventh heaven of delight.

He didn't realize he was running so fast that he could have qualified for the Olympics if this were a race. He arrived at the hospital ward without stopping. His uncle was in the staff room with a patient, telling him how to take his medicine. Anubhav was perspiring and breathing fast and stopped at once, holding on to the door.

Looking at him, his uncle stopped in the middle of his instructions.

"Anubhav, what happened to you?" his uncle asked with surprise. "Why are you breathing so fast? Is everything fine?"

"I have been selected!" Anubhav cried out joyfully. "I have been selected for Disha Technology!"

Anubhav still held onto the door frame of the staff room, beaming and looking into his uncle's eyes. He tried to breathe normally to catch his breath and gave his uncle the news one more time. "Uncle, I have been selected for Disha Technology. Sandeep has confirmed it," he said, his eyes sparkling like miniature marshmallows in a cup.

His uncle was pleased on hearing this news. He stood up from his chair and moved towards him. He hugged and praised him. Then, he took out a five hundred rupees note from his pocket and gave it to the patient sitting with him.

"You were about to go to Baniya Canteen after our meeting. Take this and bring sweets," his uncle commanded the patient sitting on the chair opposite his table. "Distribute them among the patients in the ward."

Baniya Canteen was a canteen inside the hospital premises run by a local merchant, where the patients and hospital staff were allowed to buy snacks, tea and sweets of their choice by paying for it themselves; otherwise, every patient had to follow the hospital's food and diet plan.

Anubhav reached Sandeep's office the following day and received the details of the offer and what was to be done next. Sandeep informed him that Bruno was going to issue the offer letter in a couple of days and share the joining date soon and Anubhav should be prepared to join.

There was nothing more to discuss with Sandeep and Anubhav left his office, but he was not in the mood to return to the quarter. He was not merely thrilled but utterly enraptured, as if his soul was flying on the wings of euphoria. He wanted to live in his dreams but didn't want anyone to see him. He went towards the airport, to the same broken wall and sat on it, looking towards the runway. With every flight that took off, he imagined himself sitting in it. He looked at the beaver bird's nest that was completed and from it, the chirping of the baby birds could be heard.

The bird and her little chicks were singing a living poem, a verse in the epic saga of the treetops. The air seemed to tremble with anticipation and he was listening, watching and dreaming about his new job, but he didn't know that his struggle would not end so soon.

It had been weeks but he was yet to receive the offer letter. Anubhav followed up with Sandeep every day and tried to reach out to the company and Bruno.

After a month, Sandeep informed him that Bruno was waiting for approval for these positions from the higher management before he could issue an offer letter.

"This is not usual, as the positions had been approved earlier," said Sandeep dejectedly.

There was uncertainty in Sandeep's body language and he requested Anubhav to wait for a few weeks.

Another month passed and there was still no update, so Anubhav met Sandeep again in his office.

"Bruno informed me unofficially that the company had lost the project when the hiring was at the final stage," Sandeep informed him. "Due to budget constraints, the management has not decided to release any more offer letters soon."

Anubhav's heart sank, and he was ready to dissolve into tears. His words got stuck in his throat.

"But, you need not worry," added Sandeep, looking at Anubhav's sad face. "The market is good nowadays with many new openings."

A month after the initial euphoria came the uncertainty. After being given hope, Anubhav had been deprived of a job, but it had given him a feeling of happiness that he would not feel again; it was the first punch of accomplishment. He knew that the sense of accomplishment that he had felt after being selected for Disha Technology would never arise again, however striking the success may be. Although this happiness had disappeared like a rainbow in the sun, the wild feeling of exhilaration would always be felt.

'Elation and then, deep sadness, but who knows, maybe the stars were behind it. Ridima must come to this place again,' thought Anubhav, as he tried to persuade his heart of all possible illusions.

7

DRIVING THE EFFORT ALL THE WAY

After one more setback, Anubhav found that his efforts needed to be improved, and he was required to go beyond the job postings in a weekly newspaper and a dependency on any placement consultancies. He had seen only a few companies posting job openings for freshers in newspapers or public forums. Not every placement consultancy was genuine, and many were scamming aspirants. He continuously followed up with the other two consultancies where he had registered, but they never came up with job interview, only false promises. Sandeep was helping him but that hadn't worked so far.

It had been more than six months since Anubhav had come to Pune. He had become familiar with the city and was aware of the various IT parks and company locations. He decided to visit every company, get information on open positions and ongoing recruitments and apply directly.

He had heard about Hinjewadi, a fast-growing IT hub. At least one walk-in interview from here was published weekly in the Times Ascent, but for experienced professionals. That was the right place to start.

Hinjewadi was in the north-western part of Pune. It had become one of the country's epicentres of the information technology industry.

IT companies worldwide set up their development centres there.

Anubhav boarded a bus near Pune railway station to Hinjewadi. The IT Park was far from the cantonment area and it was the longest journey he had undertaken so far within the city limits. It was about twenty miles from his place and it took more than two hours to reach there. He got off at Shivaji Chowk's bus stop near Hinjewadi. It was noon by then and the sun was directly overhead.

The place was barren, and he wondered if he was at the right place or had he boarded the wrong bus? There was a roadside shop near the bus stand where he got down. He asked the shopkeeper about the location of the Hinjewadi IT Park.

"It's nearby. Keep walking straight after taking a left at the next circle," the shopkeeper responded and showed him the path towards the road on the left.

Anubhav started walking on the road, wiping his neck with a cotton handkerchief and grimacing.

He had walked a hundred metres only when a shining multi-storey building sprang into sight. He thought from afar that it must be a major IT company, and his pace grew quick. The company's logo became visible as he reached closer to the entrance of the building. The name of the company was Persistent Systems. This was the first time he had heard of this company. Four blocks were visible inside the big campus and were named after the four Vedas – Rigveda, Yajurveda, Samaveda and Atharvaveda.

He reached the main gate and asked the security guard, "Can I go inside and meet with an HR representative?"

"Do you have an appointment?" questioned the security guard standing at the gate.

"No, I don't have an appointment. I have freshly graduated and am looking for a job here," Anubhav shared his intention.

The guard informed him that there were no recruitments currently, but he could leave his resume. Anubhav had no other choice. He handed over a copy of his resume and walked away to try his chance at the next gate.

On the opposite side, he noticed another IT giant, Infosys, in the first phase. It was the company with which he was most familiar and it was the dream of every software engineering graduate to start their career from there.

Gazing at the stringent security check, he realized that he would only be able to enter inside the gate with an appointment or by knowing anyone there. However, it didn't stop him from reaching the security guard and delivering a copy of his resume. The security desk did not only accept his resume but also shared the email address of the recruitment team.

As he walked further, he saw a grand five-star hotel, Hyatt Place. At first, he was surprised to see it and wondered what a hotel was doing there. But he could now visualize how large this IT Park was. IT companies, luxury hotels, restaurants and residential buildings were peppered throughout the campus.

He kept walking and by then, it was late afternoon. He stood on a sidewalk along the road, looking at a rainbow-coloured gate with impressive greenery. This was another IT major, Wipro Technologies, of which he had heard. He approached the security guards standing at the entrance but they told him that there were no recruitments going on for freshers. They took his resume and tossed it in a box. The box looked like a trash box rather than a drop box. He moved away, looking at them with a frown. There were many more resumes in it and he wondered if they were to be shared with the recruitment team or trashed.

Other companies were located in the same lane, like Dassault Digital and EMJ. Most of the time, the security guard was generous enough to accept his resume.

The sun was like a fireball in the sky when he had started walking towards IT Park. Its rays scorched the land, setting the glass buildings aglitter with golden sparkles. But now, the sun was a muted, wax molten-yellow, but the sunlight still poured through the walls of the buildings and reflected off the shining glass on the buildings.

He was walking along the road without food and water. He noticed an older man with a bullock cart loaded with sugarcane. The carriage was standing beside the road and he was crushing the sugarcanes using a wooden wheeled operated machine which was rotated by his bulls that were walking in a circle around it. A few IT professionals were enjoying fresh sugarcane juice. He stopped by and bought a glass of juice with mint and ice in it.

While he was drinking the juice, a city bus moved towards the Pune railway station and he realized that the day was about to end.

He looked at his watch and it was half-past five. It was time to start the tuition classes for his students, who must be waiting for him. He was late, and he had neither informed them nor his aunt that he might be late.

The park was so big that he couldn't cover it in a single day. He was still in phase one of the IT Park and two more phases remained to be visited. He had to return soon, so he decided to visit the remaining part the next day and rushed towards the nearest bus stop.

Everything he found there – the roads, the office buildings and employees – gratified him so much that he kept thinking about it. He was on a bus that was carrying him back home, but his mind was still walking on the roads of the Hinjewadi IT Park. He was applauding his judgment to come to Pune. He had reached the right place, where he aspired to work.

When Anubhav returned to the quarter, it was late and all his students had left. He used to visit some of them in their quarters to give in-house classes, but he was tired and hungry and decided not to take any tuition classes that day.

Although Anubhav was exhausted, he couldn't sleep early after he went to bed. This was because he had left the work incomplete. More than half of the Hinjewadi IT Park had been left unvisited. While trying to sleep, his mind was preparing for the next day's visit.

He woke up early in the morning, got ready and started again for Hinjewadi IT Park, without wasting any time like the previous day. He understood that it was far and needed more commuting time.

Anubhav always carried a small diary and a pen in his pocket. Whenever he was travelling to a new place or boarding a new bus, he used to write down a one-liner description of the site he planned to visit on a new page, the bus route and its number, the name of the bus stops, any change in bus service, fare and time taken to reach a destination. He had developed a pocket map that had become his travel guide. Google Maps was not available then, so the small diary was his travel guide.

With the help of his pocket map, he reached the same place the following day directly by bus. He wanted to start walking from the entry point again, where he had begun the previous day, but there were still two phases left to cover. It was a phenomenal place. The entire IT Park was spread out over more than two thousand hectares of land. He yearned to visit and submit his resume to all the companies in it.

The watch's hand was yet to touch ten. The roads were bustling as hordes of employees were reaching their offices. The youngsters were riding bikes. Their bikes looked new and were of the latest models and brands. He had not seen many of these models before and was thrilled to see them roaring around. Senior employees were using cars and many employees, particularly the female associates, were coming by auto-rickshaws and many more by company buses.

Everybody was bustling here and there, entering their offices. While observing them, Anubhav imagined how fast-moving life would be there. He kept standing near a bus stop for a while and imagined himself working in any of these offices.

"If you want to work here, you need to apply to each company," he whispered, walking towards the next shining building.

He walked along the way, talked to security guards at the gates of every company and asked about open positions, recruiter contact information or whatever they could share with him. Any information was a blessing to him. He shared his resume at every gate, even if they were not interested in accepting it, believing it would reach the company HR and their recruitment team.

Besides many big restaurants, food stalls and snack corners were set up along the road. White-collar workers were roaming around them and having tea, coffee and snacks for breakfast. Although the canteens inside the premises of every company served continental food, the roadside stalls were the favourite of many employees, particularly those who smoked. Smoking was prohibited and cigarettes were not available for purchase inside the office campus, so they had to come outside and it gave them a break from work.

Anubhav watched them closely. He stood by a snack corner where there was a crowd, staring at the people coming over and observing their identity cards. A ribbon was around their neck and a plastic card hung from it, with the name of the company printed on it. Standing at a distance, he was trying to read the name of the company and employee. He aspired to talk to them but was unsure if they would entertain him.

He observed a young man resting against a column, apart from the people, smoking a cigarette with a glassful of tea in one hand. That gentleman had looked at Anubhav once when he had come there and now looked at him again. The friendly look encouraged him to make a move.

"Good morning, sir," he addressed and greeted him warmly.

"Good morning."

"My name is Anubhav. I completed my engineering this year and am looking for a job here, but I don't know anyone who can guide me."

"Sure, what help do you need?" The gentleman was kind and encouraged him to speak. Anubhav described his challenges and mentioned needing help to find job postings for inexperienced people.

"You will not find it in newspapers. It's too difficult to manage a recruitment drive on such a large scale," said the young man, taking a puff. "Can I see your resume?"

Anubhav gave him a copy of his resume. He looked at it and returned it. Then he took out his wallet, took a business card from it and gave it to Anubhav.

"Here are my contact details. Please send your resume to my email id."

Anubhav was delighted to receive the card and thanked him. He was a senior software engineer at Infosys. Anubhav had read it on his identity card while talking to him and the same was written on his business card. His cigarette was over and he left the place, assuring Anubhav that he would get a job. Anubhav resumed walking, constantly thinking about when he would work in such a place.

8

HE WAS THE MASTER, HE WAS THE DISCIPLE

Anubhav's excitement was at its peak and he felt as though he was visiting a pilgrimage spot. He had covered over half of the Hinjewadi IT Park on foot and was still walking to cover the rest. While walking, he glimpsed a fifty-rupee note lying on the ground. He stopped and looked around to see who might have dropped it, but didn't see anyone nearby. He picked it up, thinking God wanted to reward him for his hard work, commitment and effort.

It was late noon, and he had not eaten. He looked at the note and smiled as it made for a free lunch today.

He considered having lunch in a restaurant there. While walking around and looking for a food corner, he encountered a man on the way. An eight-year-old child accompanied the man, and they both walked in his direction.

The man paused when he came closer to Anubhav and begged him, "Please help me."

"How can I help you?" inquired Anubhav.

The man narrated that he had come from Kolhapur for his son's treatment and had no money left to go back home. He begged for some money from him.

"You work in such a big company. I beg you, please help me to reach Kolhapur," the man pleaded, his eyes tearing up and glistening as they grew watery.

"I don't work here. I am looking for a job." Anubhav showed no interest in him and added, "Sorry, I don't have enough money to pay for a ticket to Kolhapur."

"Sir, please give us something, anything you like," the man begged Anubhav with folded hands. "My son has been hungry for two days."

Anubhav started thinking. He was confident that this man was playing a trick and making a fool of him. But Anubhav saw the face of the boy standing with his father, holding his father's right hand. Anubhav's heart softened.

He was also rambling here and there, looking for someone to help him, not for money or food, but to get a job. Maybe, the fifty-rupee note he had found had been given to him by god for them, so he decided to give it to them. But what if the man was lying? He chose not to give the money to him, instead he offered food.

"I can offer you lunch."

"That will also help. May god bless you," the man nodded, smiling with happiness.

At a short distance, he found a modest restaurant. The man and his son were following him. He checked the price of a lunch plate.

"Sixty rupees a plate for a vegetarian meal and seventy-five for a non-vegetarian meal," stated the owner.

He had never eaten food in a restaurant in Pune so far and was astonished to hear this. It was double the price that he was expecting. He looked at his wallet and there were two hundred rupee notes, in addition to what he had found on the way, along with a little change. It was enough to pay for two vegetarian meals.

The poor boy's eyes constantly looked at the food on the plates of others. One needed to buy a coupon and give it at another counter to get the meal. Anubhav walked towards the payment counter, ending all counter-arguments in his mind.

"Two vegetarian meals, please," he requested, taking the money from his wallet.

While the meal was being prepared, Anubhav asked the child a few questions and extracted information about them. He observed that the man had already explained to the child what to answer and remained silent himself.

Two lunch plates were ready in less than ten minutes and he handed one to the man asking, "Can you share this with your son?"

"Yes, of course. Both of us can eat it together," the man accepted. There was a plastic table and four chairs around it in the open area and they sat here, putting the plates of food on it. Anubhav took a slice of bread from his plate and put it on their plate as the two were sharing it. The man and his son started eating before Anubhav could begin.

After the meal, the man folded his hands and thanked him. Anubhav felt proud that he had been of use to someone.

Anubhav had travelled through most of the IT Park and dropped his resume in the drop box of many companies. He didn't want to miss his students like he had the day earlier, so he decided to go back home.

After walking for a distance, he reached a bus stop, but nobody was there. It was peak office hours, and the road was almost empty. Most of the employees were at work. The metal bench fixed at the bus stop was so hot that he couldn't sit on it and remained standing to wait for a bus towards MG Road.

He moved his hand to grab his pocket map to check which bus number he should board. With a shock he found that the pocket map was not in his pocket. Did he drop it on the way? He quickly moved his hands to the side pockets of his trousers and then, the upper front of the shirt to ensure that he was carrying his wallet. He checked it twice and then thrice, but couldn't find it.

The wallet was also missing. Anubhav's heart began to cry, and he checked every pocket one more time and then put down the backpack on the bench and wildly scanned inside the bag, but it was not there. He was sure he had kept both together in his back pocket. It had been there while he was buying the meal half an hour before.

Someone had picked his pocket. It must have been the man he had helped. When he took it out the last time to pay for the meals at the restaurant, the unknown man had been staring at it with the eyes of a spy.

"The man has picked my pocket!" he screamed and ran back towards the restaurant at full speed. He ran like a mad man in the middle of the road and could have hit traffic if it had been there. He entered the restaurant without stopping but couldn't locate the man.

"Did you see the man with a boy?" he questioned the person at the billing counter, breathing fast. "He had lunch here some time back."

This person didn't bother to answer him. He remained busy with his work, serving meals to his customers. Anubhav asked other people there if anyone had seen a man with a small boy. He inquired and screamed, but nobody paid any heed.

He felt pitiable and became anxious. There was no trace of the man and the boy's whereabouts. Then he sat hopelessly on a chair kept in the open area of the restaurant. He had lost two things together: a wallet and a pocket diary.

The wallet did not have money worth mourning for, but he had also lost his pocket map. It had taken him more than six months and countless trips throughout the city to prepare it. It wouldn't be possible to compile a new one. It was a pocket travel guide that he had created with dedication and he had lost it.

There was neither enough money in his wallet for the man to reach Kolhapur nor a map and route details on how to get there. The man had sinned, but this was a punishment to Anubhav for being over-generous. Although it was not a significant loss, a new wallet would make for an unplanned expenditure.

Anubhav was more than twenty miles away from his residence and had no fare to return home. He had no option but to walk to the family quarter at MH-CTC. It would take at least six to seven hours to reach home, no matter how fast he walked.

He counted every loss which was the result of this unfortunate slip. The most painful part was answering to the parents of his students as to why he had missed classes for the last two days. How much tuition fee would he get if they decided not to pay for the days of his absence? He had no excuse.

He looked at his watch. It was 3 p.m. The tuition classes were unquestionably going to be missed, and he had to start walking now if he were to reach by 9 p.m., otherwise, he would worry his uncle and aunt. They had no clue about where he was. He decided to move on and started walking towards the cantonment area of Pune city. MH-CTC was at the opposite end of this place.

He didn't stop for a single minute and kept walking without rest, water or food. The picture of the Goliber Maidan bus stop was in his mind and he was desperate to reach there as soon as possible. At the same time, his mind was still engaged in searching for the man and thinking that he would kill him if he found him. While walking quickly, he blamed himself for falling into a trap, which was a punishment that he had earned. He would never help anyone ever again.

With a thousand wild thoughts and long strides, he reached the quarter by 8:30 p.m., half an hour before he had estimated. He was tired, thirsty and hungry and his legs were hurting. He had walked through half the IT Park from morning till noon and then had returned to the quarter on foot. He had been walking for almost the entire day from 7:00 in the morning. The dinner was yet to be set and was late today, but he didn't ask for any snack or food.

He didn't mention this incident to his aunt and uncle. By the time dinner was ready, he had gone to the houses of each of his students to let them know that he had been stuck in heavy traffic and hence, couldn't reach on time. He would give them extra time the next day and requested them to be there before the usual time.

Anubhav decided to get over the unpleasant experience and move on. Despite receiving the same answers and with little hope, he continued visiting companies at Hinjewadi and other IT parks.

9

A RAY OF HOPE

Anubhav had come to Pune at the end of the previous summer and another summer was about to begin. The seasons changed, but his luck didn't and he was still searching for his dream job. His ideas and plans were like a pipe dream. There was no IT company left in the Park that he had not visited at least once. His enthusiasm waned and the eagerness to visit IT offices and meet people had substantially declined.

It had been months since he had visited the Pathfinder's office to meet Sandeep. He used to meet him at his office frequently, initially twice a week, when he would stop by there and ask him if there was any new opportunity. It was usually only a quick interaction, lasting at the most for five minutes. Now, it had been quite a few weeks since he had last visited Sandeep.

It was a Wednesday, and the sun had started rising early like before. Like every Wednesday, Anubhav's day began with buying and reading the newspaper. This time, it was not a job posting, but the astrology page that motivated him to visit Sandeep, since it contained an encouraging prediction for Cancer:

'Today, you are likely to receive a new opportunity. With the help of a person, you may have positive growth in your business or work. Your luck may help you and your losses will now turn into profits. Financial wellness may be on track now. Love birds are advised to make some important decisions in terms of marriage. Singles are likely to find their soul mate.'

Reading this reminded him of Sandeep. There was no person other than Sandeep who could have helped him. Almost two months had passed since he had met Sandeep, so he decided to meet him.

Sandeep's office was relatively smaller than the others, so the office boy would stop candidates outside in the gallery if there were already many candidates inside. When Anubhav arrived, several candidates were waiting outside, so Anubhav had to join the queue. It had been about fifteen minutes since he stood in the line before the office boy called him.

"Good morning, sir!" he greeted him. His eyes scanned the entire room. Who knows? Maybe, Ridima would be at the same place where he had seen her for the first time. Although he had met her only twice, hers was not a face that could be forgotten. Since this was the place where he had seen her for the first time, each time he came here, his eyes searched for her, although she was just in his imagination.

"Good morning, Anubhav," replied Sandeep. "It's been a long time since I have seen you. How are you doing?"

"Still the same, without a job," replied Anubhav in a gloomy tone.

Sandeep had also realized that this boy was in dire need of a job and had the least preferences and conditions.

"I have something for you," he declared.

"Would you like to consider a teaching job?"

"Teaching job, umm..." said Anubhav. He could not react since this was not a part of his dream.

"Tea... teaching," he grumbled. "What, where?"

"Don't worry. It's not a regular teaching job in a school or a college. It's a computer training institute and you need to teach the subjects of your course and essential programming languages to college-going students and young IT professionals," Sandeep revealed.

Anubhav had yet to understand what it was.

"They have a very urgent requirement. The admissions to various programs are already complete and new batches will start next month," said Sandeep.

"They must onboard the computer faculty as soon as possible and have planned job orientation for the new employees next week. There is still a position vacant for a software faculty member."

Anubhav had never thought that he would become a computer instructor instead of a computer engineer and teach programming languages in a computer institute. He kept silent, looking at Sandeep.

"You don't have much time to decide. You must go for the interview today or tomorrow at the latest as the position needs to be filled this week," said Sandeep assuredly. "I am sure that you will get this job. They are looking for a computer graduate who can teach programming languages and various academic courses."

"That's not bad, but…" Anubhav was still thinking about what to do. Changing his career goal was not an easy decision for him. He had never thought of teaching or giving computer training.

"If you don't like the job, you can always change it. I will continue sharing software engineering job postings with you." Sandeep was trying to persuade him and then, paused for a second while studying a file. "Ridima too joined here last week," he stated. It was her file in his hand.

"Ridima!" Anubhav exclaimed abruptly and then tried to look disinterested.

"Who is Ridima?" he asked, as if he did not know her.

Anubhav pretended not to know her, though she was uppermost on his mind whenever he came to this place. His eyes constantly searched for her but he was not bold enough to ask Sandeep about her.

"The girl who was shortlisted for Disha Technology along with you for the first round and both of you were called for the interview a few months back," Sandeep reminded him.

"Oh, that girl. I never saw her again. Didn't she get a job?" Anubhav wanted to gain more information about her.

"She received a couple of offers but is very picky about her career."

Anubhav desired to ask him for her mobile number but hesitated because it might give a wrong impression of him.

"You seem to be right. I should go there," Anubhav changed his mind.

"Great, that's the spirit. Can you go for the interview today? The institute is located in the Camp area. It's not too far from your place."

"Sure, sir. I can!" Anubhav was always ready to attend an interview with his resume, a copy of his degree certificate and marksheets in his backpack.

Sandeep was happy and dialled the institute in front of him. He talked to someone over the phone and notified him that he was sending a candidate.

"Anubhav is a very meritorious candidate and having a four-year degree in computer engineering, he will be perfect for your programming faculty position," Anubhav heard Sandeep recommending his name for the position.

Sandeep shared the location of the institute and the contact details of Mrs. Mani, the institute's branch manager with Anubhav and asked him to go for the interview the same day.

St. Angelo's Professional Education (SAPE) was a professional training and educational institute with multiple branches in different cities. It was hiring computer professionals to train and develop various computer and programming courses for its students and trainees.

Anubhav liked teaching but had never imagined that he would consider teaching as a career. He had dreamt of being a computer programmer, working for a multinational company and flying overseas. A change of career was not an easy decision but learning that Ridima had joined this job, made him wonder if something else was written in his fate.

Anubhav thanked Sandeep and started for SAPE, towards the JM Road Camp area. The place was not too far from the hospital quarter and he had seen the institute building and its location many times. It had never fascinated or sparked his imagination like the shining buildings of IT companies in Hinjewadi.

He was not excited about this opportunity. Instead, he was more excited about the astrology prediction he had read. Was it simply a coincidence or was everything already written in his destiny? Would he become a trainer in a computer training institute? Would he once again, meet the most beautiful girl he had ever seen and hear her melodious voice again that was still ringing in his ears?

Usually, he used to recollect answers to potential questions while going for an interview but no questions were stirring in his mind this time, except questions about fate and destiny.

His mind had so many questions running through it that the route to the institute appeared to be very short. It was noon when he reached St. Angelo's Professional Education Institute of Computer Education, located at Jangali Maharaj Road in Camp, Pune.

The lunch hour had just finished, and the employees were returning to work. As he walked towards the gate, he found an older man dressed in a dark gray safari suit and a matching Gandhian cap. The man asked him, "Are you here for admission? Which course?"

"No, I have come for an interview for a computer faculty position. Mr. Sandeep from Pathfinder job consultancy has sent me."

"Then you must be looking for Mani madam, right?"

"Yes," nodded Anubhav.

"Mrs. Mani has just come back from lunch. Let me inform her about you," the old man stood up from his seat. "What is your name?"

"My name is Anubhav Gumrah," replied Anubhav.

"Take a seat, please," he requested Anubhav, pointing towards a chair inside the office and then, walked towards a cabin.

Though he was sitting in a fully air-conditioned hall, Anubhav was still wiping his sweating face. The man returned and directed him to a cabin. Mrs. Mani had called him inside. As he moved forward, he saw a shining golden nameplate outside a room – 'Mrs. Monorma Mani Bapat, Branch Manager'. He knocked on the door and requested for permission to enter.

"Come in," a voice issued from inside the room. A plump and rosy-cheeked middle-aged woman was sitting in an easy chair with papers in her hands and thick round glasses on her eyes.

"Good afternoon. My name is Anubhav," he approached her.

"Sit down," she requested him to take a seat. "Are you Anubhav about whom Sandeep spoke?"

"Yes, madam. Sandeep has sent me here."

She asked him for his resume first, which he handed over. Then she asked him if he was carrying his degree certificate and marksheets. Anubhav was pleased to share them with her. This was the first time anyone had asked for his degree certificate. He had started believing that only the resume was required for an interview.

While looking through his documents, she asked him about his educational background and then, called someone named Mr. Kamat.

Mr. Kamat was a senior faculty member and Anubhav guessed that she had called him for technical evaluation.

"Sit down. Why are you still standing?" said the lady, noticing that Anubhav was still standing and had not taken a seat.

"Thank you, madam." He sat on the chair placed in front of her big table.

Mr. Kamat also joined them and sat in a chair next to Anubhav. She handed over his documents to him. Mr. Kamat looked at his degree and marksheets thoroughly and then asked what programming languages and subjects he could teach.

The institute had many batches of students learning programming languages and undergraduate courses. Anubhav would be eligible to teach them multiple computer subjects.

"We will pay you five thousand rupees monthly for the first three months and then evaluate your performance," announced Mrs. Mani. "Depending on the performance, we will revise your salary."

Those were magical words for him. Anubhav had got his first job offer. He was so overwhelmed that he could not understand how to react to or what to say. The compensation did not matter to him. It was the success of qualifying in the interview that sparked him. He agreed to all the terms and conditions without putting forward a single demand.

Mrs. Mani asked him to collect the offer letter the next day or Monday. She informed him that he needed to join the coming Monday, as they had planned a two-week training programme for the new faculty members and following this, several new batches would begin.

With a beaming smile that reflected a sense of accomplishment, Anubhav came out of the cabin. He paused as he stepped outside the room. Standing straight with his shoulders pulled back, he looked around the office carefully. This place was going to be his first workplace. Although his dream had not come true, he felt overjoyed.

He looked again at the people sitting there, searching for a face he had forgotten for a while. But Ridima couldn't be spotted anywhere.

As he walked outside the office, he asked the old man, "*Kaka*, how many people will be coming to join on Monday? Do you know about them?" He had heard others calling the older man Kaka.

"Only Mani madam can tell you," said Kaka, shaking his head.

Anubhav had to control his emotions and wait till Monday to see the face he yearned to see and that inspired him to change his long-standing dream.

As he came out of the office and started back home, his enthusiasm quickly waned. He recollected how crazy he had become the first time when he had received the news from Sandeep of being selected for Disha Technology. He didn't feel anything like that. He remembered the manner in which he ran to share the information with his uncle, with his feet barely touching the ground.

That inner happiness was missing this time. Anubhav was not thrilled to share this news with anybody. He walked slower than usual.

This was not a job he had been dreaming of; it was a compromise. However, it was a ray of hope in a cloud of despair. No job is insignificant, and he tried to convince himself that any work that uplifts life and provides an opportunity to live with dignity should be undertaken with painstaking excellence.

The sequence of events and Anubhav's belief in astrology made him believe that destiny had been written already. He attributed everything to the zodiac prediction he had read last week. After the successful day, when he went to his bed, it crossed his mind if the stars were behind this.

He had not imagined love and had buried this feeling deep somewhere in his heart. If the stars were behind it, was it time to meet love in his life?

Ridima's face had faded away in his memory, like seeing her through a window pane with moisture and condensation on it. Her face had now become visible again, as though someone had wiped the pane clean with a cloth.

"No, never, this cannot happen. There is a long way to walk alone," he swore to himself, before he went to sleep.

10

THE FIRST LOVE

Anubhav had got a job and had to join just three days after getting the offer. These three days passed quickly and Monday arrived. Anubhav woke up to the sound of the chirping of birds. He looked at the table clock and the alarm was yet to ring. He checked the clock to see if it was working. There was an hour more for it to ring, but the alarm was no longer needed.

Such a day didn't need an alarm to wake him. He had made up his mind to join SAPE as a staff member of the computer faculty.

Without considering the time, he left his bed and went into the bathroom. He looked at himself in the mirror and questioned himself whether he was no longer required to ask the same question he used to ask every morning, while standing in front of the mirror – 'Tell me about yourself?'

The answer to this question was wrapped in the future. But it was a changed man that was reflected in the mirror. It was the first time he could see confidence in his face and through it, he gained strength and courage. The bold man in the mirror was ready to use every small opportunity and fulfill his dreams.

Anubhav needed to report to the institute at 11 a.m., but he was ready by 8 a.m. and could hardly wait to begin work. As usual, he walked to the Goliber Maidan bus stop to board a bus, bought the newspaper daily and started reading, while sitting on the bench at the bus stop. There must be a different prediction for him that day. He turned the pages directly to read the astrology section for Cancer:

'At the beginning of the week, you will be blessed by the Lunar. You will be busy at work. Your domestic harmony will be good, which will reflect in your positive attitude. It will help you perform well at work. You will also plan for a new trade partnership. With the help of your friends or family, you will do your best. You will be able to perform well in your job, but you will demand some reward in this regard.'

He found nothing stimulating, but this didn't disappoint him. He boarded the bus number 90 for the institute.

He reached before time and the institute was yet to open. He knew he would arrive before time but he had the newspaper with him to kill time. He found a suitable place near the institute gate and started going through the pages of the newspaper. It was a quarter to ten when the same old man called Kaka, came and unlocked the main gate of the office.

"Good morning, Kaka," Anubhav greeted the old man, walking towards the office gate.

"Good morning, sir. You must be joining today."

"Yes, today is my first day."

"The staff arrives by 11 a.m. You can sit inside," the old man informed him.

He helped Kaka open the big shutter gate of the institute.

"Sir, don't bother. It's my daily job," the old man insisted. "Please take a seat inside. I will get tea for you." Saying this, he went outside to order tea at a nearby corner shop.

Anubhav sat on a sofa inside. There was nobody there except for him and Kaka. Kaka had already ordered two cups of tea from a tea seller outside. Soon, a young boy entered with two cups of tea. Anubhav thanked both of them.

Half an hour passed and Anubhav watched the movements inside the office which had just begun. The staff and students started arriving gradually, and the institute was half full in the next hour. Mr. Kamat was one of the first persons to arrive. He informed Anubhav about the joining process and mentioned that four more faculty members would join him. He needed to wait for them before the joining formalities started.

Anubhav guessed that one of them would be Ridima and was impatient to meet her. By 11 a.m., three more colleagues joined Anubhav and Mr. Kamat invited them into a room. The fourth newcomer was missing and Ridima didn't show up. His heart broke.

Anubhav had been told that four more people would join him, but apart from him, only three others had reported. He had decided to consider a teaching opportunity only because of her, but she was not present.

'Did she get another opportunity?' Anubhav could only wonder.

There was no way of knowing it. He felt sad at not being able to see her, but the happiness of joining his first job was no less than meeting a soulmate. All the astrology predictions need not be correct. He prayed for her and thanked god for the opportunity given to him.

The new faculty introduced themselves. Two of the candidates were men, Neel and Vinod. Both were old friends and had previously worked as corporate trainers in an MNC. They both looked much older and were about forty-five years old. The third person was a lady named Nina. She also had rich experience in teaching and had moved here from another institute in a different city. Mr. Kamat gave them a few forms to fill out and requested the necessary documents for employee verification, identification, bank account details, etc.

A couple of hours passed and Anubhav and the other three completed filling out the given forms. They talked to each other about their experiences and how they had reached there. A long time passed, and they were waiting for the staff to come and give further instructions.

The door opened abruptly, and a face appeared like sunlight shining through the gaps in the clouds. Ridima was standing behind the half-open door. Everyone in the room stopped talking and looked at her.

"Hi," she said, waving her hand towards them.

Though the others were calm, Anubhav almost stopped breathing. He felt his heartbeats become so loud that the room seemed too small to mask them.

He needed a way to control his racing emotions. He controlled himself and tried to become calm before anyone could notice him.

"Hi," he raised his hands and waved towards her.

Looking at Anubhav, she stopped and stood still for a while. They looked at each other and the shock on her face was more evident than that of Anubhav, although she had met him a few times. A twinkle came into her eyes and she smiled. Anubhav hesitated to stare at her continuously. Before it could make her uncomfortable, he broke eye contact with her and looked straight towards the whiteboard on the wall.

Ridima walked inside the room and pulled a chair next to him. He couldn't believe it. There were five rows in the room and he was sitting alone in the third row. Neel and Vinod were seated in the first row, while Nina was on the other side of the second row. Ridima chose to sit next to him.

"I can't believe this. You are also here," said Ridima with a laugh.

"Yes, I am here. Can't I teach students?"

"No, I didn't mean that, but..."

"But I was expecting to see you here," Anubhav interrupted her. "Sandeep informed me that you would be joining this institute as a computer faculty."

"Oh, I see. But you were selected for Disha Technology. Didn't you join that company?" she probed, surprised.

"I have not gotten a joining date from them till today," Anubhav replied and there was pain on his face.

"I am sorry to hear this," said Ridima, feeling pity for him.

"You don't need to be sorry. Maybe, I am destined to work here with you," remarked Anubhav, giving a fake laugh.

The door opened again. It was Mr. Kamat this time. It was lunchtime, but nobody had informed the newcomers, so he apologized.

"It's lunchtime and you can take a break for one hour and have your lunch. There is a dining area if you have brought your lunch box or you can go outside. There are many good restaurants alongside the market street," Mr. Kamat directed them.

Neel, Vinod and Nina had brought lunch boxes with them and went to the dining area. Since Ridima had been late and still needed to complete the paperwork, she continued completing the formalities.

Anubhav came outside for a meal. Jangali Maharaj Road was a very famous and posh market area in Pune. There were shops, roadside stalls and many good restaurants located there. He walked alongside the road and looked for a place offering ample food at the lowest price.

He found a roadside food stall at a distance that served a full plate meal at a reasonable price – a vegetarian meal for forty rupees and a non-vegetarian meal for fifty rupees per plate. It was cheaper than the one he had eaten the last time in Hinjewadi and had an unlimited quantity. There were no sitting arrangements, like in a regular restaurant, but several plastic chairs were arranged alongside the road. The food items were stored in a movable trolley with no cover.

Many people, particularly daily wage workers working there in construction and other menial work were standing and eating along the footpath with plates in their hands.

Anubhav ordered a vegetarian meal. The lady filled an empty plate with rice, lentil soup, curry and six chapattis. There could not be any place cheaper than this and Anubhav had found a place for lunch. He enjoyed the food and though it didn't taste very good, it was more than enough.

Only half an hour of the break had passed, so he roamed the streets, observing every shop and place in the area. He found this place attractive. Though the office was not as striking and modern as an IT company, its location was one of the best.

Everybody was back in the room after the lunch break. Mr. Kamat joined them again and shared the schedule for the next two weeks.

"There are two weeks of training and orientation planned. It would be best if you prepared yourself to teach different batches. The batch details and time will be shared later," he instructed the newly joined staff members.

"Remember, there is a dress code for all staff members; all men need to wear a formal dress with a tie and ladies can wear a western or Indian formal dress," Mr. Kamat finished the briefing for the day. He was also wearing formal trousers, shirt and a tie.

Hearing about the dress code, Anubhav became uneasy and the smile on his face disappeared. He lost the confidence that he had developed so far. He had only one pair of formal shirts, pants and a single tie that he had bought for an interview.

The joining formalities were completed, and they were now free.

All four of them came outside together and said goodbye to each other. Neel and Vinod were local homeowners and used to ride bikes, while Nina rode a scooter. So, the three of them went towards the parking area of the building to get their vehicles. Anubhav and Ridima walked outside the building premises to look for public transportation.

"You live in the cantonment area, right," asked Ridima as they reached an auto-rickshaw that was waiting for a passenger along the street. She still remembered that.

"Yes, I live there."

"Which side is it and how far?" she asked, unaware of the exact location of MH-CTC.

"It's next to your place," said Anubhav, without a second thought.

"Oh, then we can share the ride. I will get down near my apartment at Kothrud and you can continue from there," said Ridima, suggesting a shared ride.

MH-CTC was in the reverse direction of Kothrud from this place, but Anubhav told her the opposite. He had regretted not accepting her offer to share an auto-rickshaw ride in the past.

"Driver, will you please go to Kothrud?" she asked the auto-rickshaw driver, who had pulled down the metre before she could say anything. She got into the auto-rickshaw.

"We will share the fare," she told Anubhav, dispelling his doubt about who would pay the fare.

It would take him in the opposite direction from his place and be an expensive trip. But Anubhav couldn't decline the offer this time. He had met this girl a few months back and her face was etched in his memory. After a short meeting, she had disappeared like a cloud in the sky and had now appeared again. She was sitting next to him, laughing, giggling, smiling and talking. His mind still needed to decide if this was a dream or reality.

He was clueless about what to say and reflect. He hadn't been prepared for such a situation in his life. Half an hour passed, and he only answered the questions she was asking and didn't ask her anything in return. Silently, Anubhav thanked his fate and the position of the stars.

The auto-rickshaw reached in front of an apartment building.

"Please stop at the gate," she directed the driver to stop and then asked about the fare to be paid. "How much is the fare?"

"Fifty rupees, madam."

She took out a fifty-rupee note and gave it to the driver.

"Bye-bye. See you tomorrow," Ridima waved a hand towards Anubhav, who was still contemplating if he should stop her from paying the driver.

"Continue to MH-CTC family quarters," he told the auto-rickshaw driver after waving goodbye to her.

The auto-rickshaw had not even moved a hundred metres before the building and place where Ridima had got down was out of sight. Anubhav changed the plan spontaneously.

"Please stop. I need to get down," Anubhav conveyed to the driver.

As the auto-rickshaw stopped, he stepped down and told the driver that he no longer needed it. The driver looked at him as though he had robbed him of his day's earnings and said in an irritated tone, "You should have got down there with madam. Why did you say you had to continue towards MH-CTC?"

Anubhav didn't want to do this but if he could manage to reach home in five rupees in a bus, it was not wise to spend fifty rupees travelling in an auto-rickshaw.

When happiness comes to one's door, it comes not only in one, but many ways. Anubhav had got a job and met his dream girl on the first day. Another good message was waiting for him when he returned to the quarter.

His uncle informed him that he had received a call from one of his kin who had been transferred to Hyderabad recently. He had helped him through school and college.

"He has asked you to join him in Hyderabad. He has a few friends there working in IT companies and he will try to find something for you," stated his uncle.

Anubhav had spent about nine months staying with his uncle in Pune and worried that he may be uncomfortable. He should have left long ago and lived independently, but hadn't been able to do so.

Though he had gotten a job now, it was not paying enough to rent a house and live independently. He had visited every IT company he could spot in the city but to no avail. He had no hope of getting a job of his choice. There was no company left that he could think of and apply to, and he was sick and tired of looking for an IT job in Pune.

Listening to his uncle, he danced with joy. "I will move to Hyderabad now and look for a job there," he said without giving it a second thought.

But instantly, he regretted his decision. It was the beginning of a new chapter for him and what had happened had never happened before. A zodiac astrology prediction had come true for him. There was reason to believe that one's destiny was written and the stars drive a person's life. He was hoping that his career path would come from a teaching job. He wanted to stay for some more time in Pune and continue the teaching job at the computer training institute.

For the first time, his heart won over his mind.

Anubhav reached the office at exactly eleven on the second day, dressed formally with a tie.

Kaka was sitting on a plastic chair at the main gate. "Good morning, sir," he greeted Anubhav.

It was the first time anybody had greeted him in that manner. Till that day, he used to address everybody as 'sir' and say good morning or good evening first, be it an employee, security guard or a peon.

Admittedly, he felt like an officer for the first time, though he responded humbly like before, "Good morning, Kaka. How are you doing today?"

Kaka's face lit up as no one had ever asked about his wellness before.

Everyone was already present in the room when he entered. As usual, Neel and Vinod were sitting together and talking to each other. Nina was discussing something with Ridima and both were sitting in the same place as the previous day. Anubhav joined them and took the same chair beside Ridima, where he had sat the previous day. Their chairs remained fixed for the next week of the training.

After a while, Mr. Kamat entered the room, but he was not alone. He was following Mrs. Mani, and she was walking ahead of him like his boss.

"Good morning, madam. Good morning, sir," everyone in the room greeted them in unison.

Mr. Kamat greeted them back but Mrs. Mani didn't pay any attention to them and didn't respond either. Instead, she put her purse on the table loudly, almost tipping it over and immediately started on her agenda. She explained the rules and regulations for the employees and the policies of the institute in a stern voice.

"She is behaving like a school headmaster," Ridima whispered into his ear, pushing herself so close that he could feel her breathing.

"Of course, she is one," Anubhav rejoined in the same vein. "You have joined a coaching institute and are going to teach here."

With a grimace, she pulled herself away from him, looked straight towards Mrs. Mani and both of them chuckled.

Mrs. Mani continued speaking non-stop, without giving a chance to anyone to ask a single question. At last she said, "Mr. Kamat will answer all your questions."

It took her one and a half an hour to finish her address before she left the room without looking at any of them individually. It was then that the room came alive again and there was some noise in it.

"It is lunchtime. Please go and have your lunch. We don't schedule classes between 12:30 p.m. and 1:30 p.m. so that everyone can enjoy their lunch. See you later," saying this, Mr. Kamat, too, left the room.

Nina, Vinod and Neel lived with their families and carried their lunch boxes like the previous day. They requested that Anubhav and Ridima join them.

"Thank you, I like to eat outside," said Anubhav, as it would be a daily routine and he had found a place for himself.

Surprisingly, Ridima echoed him, "I also want to eat outside."

She joined him as she was not carrying a lunch box. Anubhav didn't expect this.

"I like this place. There are many good restaurants," said Ridima, as they walked along the road outside the office building.

Anubhav felt nervous about being with a girl at lunchtime. He couldn't go to a place with poor arrangements, where food was served in the open area on the roadside. The fact that Ridima was accompanying him at lunchtime had placed him in a terrible dilemma. He hadn't imagined such a situation.

"Which restaurant did you go to yesterday? Shall we go there?" she asked again when she didn't receive any reply from him for a long time. She was the only one talking so far.

"I went to a restaurant far from here and the food was not good. We shall try another one." He was unwilling to disclose that he had chosen the cheapest food in this area and would have gone there again if she hadn't joined him.

"I liked Shiv Sagar. Its food is delicious, and it's the best vegetarian restaurant in this area," she said. Ridima was a vegetarian. Anubhav had yet to experience eating outside in a quality restaurant.

After walking for fifteen minutes, they reached Shiv Sagar restaurant.

A person wearing a traditional dress and a tall hat welcomed them, "Good afternoon, sir, good afternoon, madam, welcome to Shiv Sagar!"

"It is noon, and the restaurant is not fully occupied. In the evening, one has to wait in a queue to get a table here," said Ridima.

They settled in their seats and a waiter came with two glasses of water and handed menus to them. Anubhav looked at the prices quoted on the right side. However, he was determined to swim in the river stream like a straw, without caring which way he was carried.

"You have tried it before, so you know what to order here," he placed the menu back on the table.

"Are you sure?" she questioned him.

"Yes, I will go with your choice. I know it is going to be sweet like you."

"Oh, is that so? Do not blame me later," she shrieked with laughter and their eyes met as though they were seeing each other for the first time.

Though Anubhav and Ridima were no longer strangers to each other, it was the first time he got an opportunity to talk to her naturally and without bothering about the time. Ridima was sitting on the opposite side of the table before him. He could look at her continuously and without any hesitation.

Ridima was quick to place the order. Anubhav could only respond, "Same," when the waiter asked his choice.

"You seem to be very hungry," Ridima said without hesitation. "You are not talking about anything and are looking at the food and restaurant like you haven't seen them before."

She was correct, unaware that Anubhav had never been to such a lovely restaurant. He wanted to speak the truth but kept it to himself. He didn't want to share the helplessness and adversities he was going through.

She was smiling at everything, at each question and every answer. Her every action started with a smile that had become more natural, unlike the first takeaway smile and blooming more than before.

Anubhav had hardly had anything of his choice so far, but the princess of his dreams was sitting before him. He realized that the world was full of uncertainties and a miracle had happened to him.

It was the second day of training and they had to be punctual. Finishing lunch, they walked quickly back to the office. The other three were already in the room and Mr. Kamat had just entered. He distributed the training material and information about the resources like the library and curriculum material. In a week or two, they were to commence taking classes. They could use the library, computer, internet and other resources to prepare for classes.

At the end of the day, he shared an auto ride with Ridima like the previous day and got down at the same place after dropping her off outside her apartment building and then looked for a city bus.

11

THE HAPPIEST MOMENTS

The first week passed satisfactorily, learning new procedures and making new acquaintances as a faculty member in a computer institution. The job orientation was completed. Though it had been planned for two weeks originally, the new batches started earlier than anticipated. The new trainers got assigned classes and subjects to teach as per their qualifications and expertise.

Vinod, Neel and Nina had experience in teaching programming languages, so they would train professionals. Anubhav and Ridima were engineering graduates, so they were assigned classes to develop engineering subjects for students who had joined the institute for improvement in the academic subjects of their engineering courses. Most of these students were not from the computer engineering branch and had enrolled to learn computer engineering subjects outside their universities.

Though the financial situation remained the same for Anubhav, his days had changed. On the professional side, it was more restful and appealing than the initial six days of training. There were only a few batches of engineering classes as the additional batches still had to start. So, both Ridima and he had only two groups to teach for two hours each day and they were free for the rest of the day. However, all permanent staff members were expected to be in the office from 11 a.m. to 8 p.m. to mark a full day's attendance.

During the first few days, Anubhav spent the remaining hours in the library and the computer lab. The library was small and had limited books of his interest, but the computers in the training lab had many advantages. Each computer was connected to the internet, with perfect surfing speed, since the institute had a high-speed broadband line. He had not observed such speed anywhere outside an internet cafe before and he was accessing high-speed internet for the first time.

After Ridima, the computer and the internet appealed to him the most. He had the privilege to access any computer with unlimited internet, which was a bonus for him. Before this job, he only accessed the internet in a cyber cafe for a few hours a week. The limited plan of twenty hours that he purchased in an internet cafe in Mira market was good only for checking job requirements and sending emails. He spent these twenty hours carefully. Just like the money from his pocket.

Anubhav had become aware of the internet's potential now. Information about all the companies was available on the net, including their job postings and contact details. However, he still needed help in finding a job opening for a fresher or a person with lesser experience.

The internet world was relatively new to Anubhav, and it appealed so much to him that it triumphed over his attraction towards Ridima for a few days.

However, he was so involved that he would always be counting the hours till lunch. His eyes were on the clock constantly, waiting for noon.

Ridima and Anubhav used to go outside together to have lunch, which allowed them to talk and get to know each other. For the first few days, they were back in an hour which was the allotted lunchtime, but slowly, as time went by, they started leaving for lunch much earlier and returned only when their classes were about to start and the students had assembled in the classroom.

After a month, they started going outside during lunch and tea breaks, if there was no class scheduled. Tea was served on the table twice a day and they could order snacks or lunch like the others; instead, they preferred going outside.

As the days passed, Anubhav and Ridima were outside most of the time and were visible in the institute only during their class timings. They visited all the restaurants located there, every ice-cream and snack corner. They explored all the nearby parks and gardens, frequently visited Saras Baug and remained sitting under a tree until it was time for classes or they needed to sign off on the register for the day.

They spent most of the day together, started liking each other's company and began ignoring the others in the institute. Their presence in the institute was limited only to the classroom.

There was no end to their conversations. Ridima wanted to talk about movies, dance and theatre, while Anubhav only shared a few hobbies. She was a classical dancer and competed in national contests. He didn't know much about movies and theatre.

A hobby comes with spending money. Life had not offered him a day to enjoy anything; only misery and poverty. Anubhav discovered for the first time that life was not only about misfortunes and blues. Despite all its trouble, drudgery and broken dreams, there was a beautiful world that remained hidden from him.

It was a Saturday when Anubhav and Ridima were sitting under a tree in a nearby park.

Suddenly, Ridima asked, "Shall we meet tomorrow?"

"Hmm... but why? Is there a class scheduled?" countered Anubhav.

"Why... means? Do you have any fun or are you only interested in classes?" she inquired furiously.

"I mean, what is special tomorrow?" defended Anubhav.

"Shahrukh's new movie has been released – *Veer Zara*. I want to see that and I am bored with eating at the same restaurants here," she said as if to taunt him that she had to say this to him after talking about Shahrukh and his movies for days. Shahrukh Khan was her favourite actor, and she didn't miss a single film. She would rewatch his movies any number of times. Mostly, she watched his movies first-day first-show, but this job had broken her record, and she had missed the new film.

While this was usual for her, it was not an ordinary affair for Anubhav. He didn't have the courage to ask her to go to a movie or have dinner. He was mindful of his position on the social ladder, but nowadays, his heart and mind were in a strange world with no roads and traffic to navigate, only the rising desires. There was only a whirlwind of stormy winds laden with perfumes in which he was swinging.

Anubhav and Ridima planned to watch a 6 p.m. show at Inox Cinema in Bund. It was 8 p.m. and the institute would be closing. They had not shown their faces at the end of the day.

"We have missed reporting back at work and didn't sign the register," he said, concerned. "What will we say?"

"You fret too much. We will find an answer. Let's think about the movie," she insisted. Her face had no signs of anxiety and she only cared about the new film of her favourite actor.

Anubhav couldn't sleep that night. His heart was racing like someone was stoking the fire with bellows. He was wandering in a dream land full of gardens with blossoming flowers. Butterflies were resting on them, birds were humming all around, winds were blowing in all directions and he could feel the fragrance of each bud, plant and tree. At the same time, his mind was worrying about what to wear the next day.

When he woke up in the morning, he looked at his limited set of clothes. There were better choices than the pair of formal trousers and shirts he used to wear daily to work. There was another pair – a maroon shirt and brownish trousers. It was an old but a designer shirt and he had not worn it to the office.

He cleaned and ironed it. He bathed twice that day, once in the morning and then in the evening, before getting ready. He was aware that his body sweated a lot. He sprinkled Dermi Cool talcum powder all over his body and applied double on the parts where he would sweat.

He had already polished his black shoes using Cherry Blossom boot polish during the day. They shone so much that one could see one's reflection in them. He looked at the mirror for the last time. He was not a cowboy but a gentleman full of vitality and freshness.

He didn't walk to the Goliber Maidan bus stop this time but waited for an auto-rickshaw outside the hospital security gate, unlike other times. He wanted to avoid the crowd on the bus as it could mess up the pleats of the shirt and fade the shine of the shoes. Besides, who could predict rain in Pune? Though it was a pleasant day, there was a risk of his clothes getting dirty. The rainy season had just begun.

It was a Sunday during the monsoon season and it was drizzling intermittently. The shuddering gusts of rain, soaked with the smell of the earth, turned the city into a fairyland of nature.

There was such a wind around, such smell that a fairy was bound to come. Who wouldn't be lured and so was the young boy from a small village. A miracle had happened to him.

He reached the place where Ridima lived but didn't find her outside. He stopped suddenly and became suspicious. A thought struck his mind. Ridima was fond of fun and play. Could it be that this was a prank and he would be the subject of a joke in the office the next day?

It is tough to believe in immense happiness when you can't remember the last time when you were happy. Anubhav looked at his watch instantly; it was just past five, and he had arrived early. He cursed himself for his weakness of always being negative and asking the auto-rickshaw driver to wait for five minutes, and rushed to her apartment on the second floor.

He rang the bell twice in one minute. The door didn't open. He was about to ring it again, but by doing so would be considered rude. So he decided to wait for some more time.

The door opened in less than five minutes and as the door opened, Anubhav almost stopped breathing and his heart fluttered. Ridima was standing behind the door looking like a red rose that had just blossomed from a fragrant bud. She looked gorgeous in a red boutique salwar suit in raw silk with its round neckline embellished with mirrors, sequins and *zari* and crafted with pearls. A teardrop red ruby surrounded by shining diamonds, fitted in a golden pendant was gleaming on her neck. The matching earrings, pear-shaped bold red rubies with glittering diamond halos were hanging from her ears. Her charcoal hair was loose and fell to her waist and her cream sandals contrasted with her dress. She looked like an angel descended from heaven.

Anubhav lost all sense and stood like a statue. He kept looking at her without any fear of being called rude. He didn't care if she noticed him and what she would think of him.

"Shall we not go now?" she said in a low tone, like someone attempting to wake a person from a night of sleep.

"We have to wait in a queue to get the tickets," she was a bit louder this time.

Anubhav recovered his senses and her smirk showed that his hard work had paid off. There was another coincidence; his dress matched hers.

"I have already got the tickets," he replied, taking two movie tickets from his pocket and surprising her.

There was a chance of the tickets being sold out and not be available in the evening. Anubhav didn't want to miss this opportunity, so he had visited the theatre in the morning when it opened and bought two tickets. Movie tickets were not available online in those days.

"Wow. That's wonderful! You are superb, Anubhav, oh... my SRK," Ridima exclaimed, lowering her gaze.

Holding both the tickets in her hand, Ridima rushed towards a table inside the room and took her handbag. They were ready to go.

As they exited the building, dark clouds covered the sky. Though it was not raining heavily, large raindrops started falling on their head, eyelids and hands.

The auto-rickshaw was waiting outside, and they ran towards it. Ridima got in first and then Anubhav sat on her left side. He instructed the driver to go to Inox, Bund Garden.

As the speed of the auto-rickshaw increased, it started raining. The atmosphere was filled with the fragrance of the moist, soft earth. The trees flanking the road were transformed into musical instruments, their branches playing the delicate pitter-patter as if conducting a celestial choir. Like musical notes, the raindrops played a sonorous tune as they caressed the leaves.

Her perfume was a mysterious blend of spices and vanilla and it wafted around, filling the auto-rickshaw. Her hair, blown by the wind, smelt of jasmine. The droplets splashing on her cheeks were glistening. The spots on her dress where the drops fell had become darker in colour, contrasting with her fair skin. It seemed like Mother Nature had turned into an artist for her daughter.

Ridima was silent and calm, looking straight towards the road. Anubhav was dumbfounded and gazed continuously at her face.

They didn't talk to each other during the entire journey. Ridima stayed silent and Anubhav turned to his left outside the auto-rickshaw towards the road. He was trying to catch the falling raindrops in his hand and counting as many as he could. He was thinking about what would have happened to this poor gentleman if the rain hadn't been there. He would have been consumed in a fever of admiration.

Not a single word was exchanged and the auto-rickshaw reached the theatre and stopped in the parking area inside, which Anubhav didn't realize until it stopped. They got down and he paid the driver. The last show had just ended, and the crowd was coming out of the cinema hall as they went inside. The next show was about to start.

"It looks like the show will begin soon," said Anubhav, trying to break the long silence.

The entry gate was open and people were rushing in for the show. They followed the crowd.

The show began with the national anthem. Ridima was sitting in the seat right next to him. Though cool air was blowing through the centralized air conditioner in the theatre, Anubhav was sweating. The lights were turned off as the movie was about to start. He took a handkerchief from his pocket and wiped his eyes and forehead. He was grateful for the rain outside once again, because of which, nobody could notice he was sweating.

It was the first time he would be watching a movie in a multiplex and that too, with the girl of his dreams. Otherwise, his movie adventures were confined to the open-air theatre of the MH-CTC cinema hall that was free for the patients, hospital staff and their families.

He was stunned to see the theatre and its screen. 'Does every multiplex happen to be like this or is it one of its kind?' he mused.

Every new place and new artwork excited him like a kid, but the cinema hall was not the only thing worth examining. The most challenging task was dealing with the extraordinary feeling he had been going through for more than an hour. He shifted his attention from the theatre to the virtue of his fortune.

He didn't want any part of his body to touch hers inadvertently. At the same time, he knew that the odour of his sweat was offensive, so he tried to keep an adequate distance to avoid any contact with Ridima. The movie started, and he was sitting in a velvet-padded seat, folding his hands and arms on his chest carefully.

When you are extra cautious and circumspect, mistakes are inevitable. Anubhav unfolded his arms, shifting his position on the chair to relieve a cramp and something unwelcome occurred. He kept his right hand on the armrest and it came into contact with someone else's hand. Ridima was already resting her hand on it.

He pulled his hand back with electrifying speed. While he felt guilty, he realized she wasn't bothered about it and there was no reaction from her side. He thought that there wouldn't be a coward like him.

After some time, he found that her hand was still in the same place. A mummified feeling inside him was unwrapping gradually. His heart repeatedly told him that it was now or never.

He closed his eyes, held his breath and gathered as much courage as possible. He placed his right hand on Ridima's hand, trying to catch it. She waited momentarily and then, slowly pulled her hand from his grasp. Anubhav's sixth sense was tipped off. Was she offended?

He should not have done this to her. It wouldn't be easy to look into her eyes once the light was turned on. His mind was filled with guilt. He wanted to apologize for his misbehaviour but couldn't think of how to go about it.

But then, an incredible thing happened. Ridima leaned towards him, gently rested her head on his shoulder and twisting her right hand, held his right arm. The guilt that had just overshadowed his mind, faded in the dark hall filled with the changing lights from the projector.

His heartbeat was lost in the surrounding sound of music. He closed his eyes and stopped breathing one more time, leaving no room for doubt in his mind.

Then, he moved his right hand towards her hand, still resting on the same armrest and held it, interlocking his fingers with hers. Their hands met like old friends reuniting, each finger weaving a tale of unspoken affection. It felt like he was holding warm rose petals in his hand. He had never felt anything like this before.

Anubhav had come to watch a movie in a multiplex for the first time, but he didn't know when it ended. He had read its title and could remember its soundtrack, but that was all that he could remember. He had a different film running through his mind.

The movie ended and everybody went outside. Finding themselves left alone, Anubhav and Ridima stood up and walked silently outside the theatre.

"I am feeling hungry," said Anubhav, trying to act normal. "Where shall we go for dinner?"

"We will go," she responded with a smile. "But I will pay this time."

Anubhav had already bought the movie tickets and paid for the auto-rickshaw trip, so dinner was on her.

"Sure, why not?"

"Maratha Samrat," she returned swiftly.

They started walking along the bustling street. The restaurant was not far away and as they entered it, the manager welcomed them and said promptly, "A candlelight dinner, sir?"

Ridima kept silent and gave no reaction, but the natural smile on her face was missing.

Anubhav replied quickly, "No, we need a regular table."

Looking at her, Anubhav was convinced that Ridima had not heard the beats of hundreds of drums in his heart and he didn't want to give any indication of it.

It was a busy restaurant, but they didn't need to wait and soon got a table for two. Soon, a delicious dinner was on their table, which was of Anubhav's choice.

If you crave something, have it. He had found a once in a lifetime opportunity to have dinner that he could only dream of and wanted to satisfy all his desires.

"We will have dessert outside," expressed Anubhav, as the dinner was about to end. "There are good ice-cream shops in this area." He wanted to have his favourite ice-cream with her.

Ridima screamed with joy, "I love ice-cream!" She was so delighted that she immediately forgot about Shahrukh.

"I would have taken you to an ice-cream shop right after the movie if I had known this earlier. One ice-cream could have saved me from a stuttering biography."

"Don't joke about Shahrukh. I am not in a mood to beat you," threatened Ridima with a burst of laughter.

The streets were bright, with the light of sodium lamps on both sides. But the crowd had dispersed, and the moon climbed into the sky. It was getting late in the night, so after buying ice-cream from an ice-cream shop that was closing for the day, they hailed an auto-rickshaw to go to Kothrud, her residence.

The ice-cream was over soon and the auto-rickshaw ran at full speed. There was hardly any traffic left and all the shops' shutters on both sides of the busiest market were down. No one was walking on the road and all the roadside stalls were closed.

There was silence once again, carrying the bittersweet resonance of the music that had touched their souls. Both riders sat silently in the auto-rickshaw as if they didn't know each other. The auto-rickshaw reached her apartment building in less than half an hour.

"Please stop," said Ridima, guiding the auto driver.

"Good night," she said calmly, just audible enough to be heard between them.

"Good night," he acknowledged, coming out of his world.

She got down from the auto-rickshaw without saying anything. She stopped after walking five steps and looked back towards Anubhav with a strange look as if trying to convey a message to him without words.

It was midnight and nobody was present. The lights of all the apartments in the building were switched off. Anubhav realized his mistake; he should have accompanied her to the gate and let her inside the building.

He stepped off the auto-rickshaw quickly and approached her. He found the world outside the auto-rickshaw to be entirely different from before.

The clouds in the sky had disappeared, giving way for the stars to twinkle all over the sky. The gusts of wind in the evening had stopped as if resting on the leaves of trees. The neighbourhood was quiet, though the airconditioners on the windows of the apartments were whirring, suppressing the constant buzz of crickets.

Ridima, who was standing a couple of feet away at the same place, was in front of him. Coming closer, he looked at her eyes and face and, at last, above at the sky.

The bright full moon was shining behind her, as though she was wearing a silver crown on her head. Twinkling stars had got entangled in her loose hair. The diamonds of her pendant and earrings caught the moonlight. Her face was glowing whiter than ever before, like the colour of a swan in the moonlight.

He stood there without breathing. Looking at Ridima, a question came to his mind.

Who was more beautiful, the moon above in the sky or the moon before him on the ground? He was looking at both continuously at the same time and trying to find an answer. Ridima kept standing like a statue at the centre of a palace.

Suddenly, the barking of faraway dogs broke the silence in the air and a dark cloud appeared from somewhere and covered the moon. Anubhav came out of his trance and moved forward to open the building's main gate, as there was no guard present. Ridima followed him and entered the gate as he opened it.

"Bye," she said in a soft voice, waving her hand from the other side of the gate.

"Bye-bye and have a good night," returned Anubhav, closing the gate.

As he turned back, he looked at the sky one more time. The cloud disappeared magically, and the moon shimmered again, as though smiling at him.

He returned to the auto-rickshaw waiting on the road with its engine still running.

Shortly, he was sitting alone in the auto-rickshaw, which had taken a turn and was speeding towards the MH-CTC family quarters. The question, however, was still in his mind: who was more beautiful, the moon in the sky or the moon on the ground?

The moon in the sky had shady spots, but the second was flawless – elegant, prettier and full of empathy, compassion and affection.

As he answered one question, another question arose in his mind. Would he become a dark spot in her life and diminish her beauty like those on the moon did?

Before he could figure out an answer to this question, the auto-rickshaw entered the hospital compound and stopped in front of the quarter.

The happiest moments in life come in the darkest season of time and Anubhav discovered this truth. He had forgotten all the pain and suffering that he was going through for a moment. At the same time, he was scared that somebody might cast an evil eye on his happiness.

12

SLIPPING APART

There were other girls in the institute, but no one was like Ridima. Everybody admired her beauty, from the staff to the students and she was a topic of conversation. Everybody was desperate to get a glimpse of her from the first day. Their relationship had become a subject of discourse in every corner of the institute. The other staff members observed them and whispered to each other whenever they were seen together.

Ridima didn't bother with such things, but for Anubhav, it was different and a touchy subject. He had been an extremely self-conscious person. He felt that everybody was watching his every move and judging him. If he saw two or more people speaking together, he was sure they were talking about him and if any one of them looked in his direction, it was just the confirmation that his battered psyche needed in order to feel even more self-conscious. Maybe, his upbringing had made him like that.

Ridima was with him for the most part of the day and he was sure that someone was watching him almost all the time, even when he was alone.

The next day, something would happen that would change both his address and his path for the future.

Anubhav and Ridima spent most of their time outside the institute together. It became an eyesore for many and had also reached Mrs. Mani's ears. Nobody directly commented about their relationship, but their dedication towards their work and commitment was challenged.

Anubhav and Ridima never missed any class, nor were they ever late to start it. Their students were happy with how they were teaching, but they stayed outside the institute if no class was scheduled.

Unfortunately, they didn't show up after the class and at the end of business hours on the last day, so a complaint was pending the next day. It gave everyone the chance they had been waiting for.

Every other staff member took four to five classes a day, but the batches of the engineering subjects were limited and the young trainers had only two batches assigned to them. It would not be incorrect to say that many staff members were jealous of their relationship and lesser work.

The next day, a staff meeting was called to address the complaint filed against them. Mrs. Mani made a new rule and instructed that every staff member be present on the institute premises during business hours except lunchtime, irrespective of whether they have any class scheduled or not.

She left the room without specifying any name or pinpointing anyone, but it was apparent to who she was pointing. Listening to her, Anubhav became nervous. His odd behaviour seemed to encourage Vinod, who was a bully by nature and left no opportunity to humiliate Anubhav. "What will the teacher in school uniform do now?" he said, looking towards Anubhav.

He called Anubhav a student as he used to dress in the same pair of clothes daily. Anubhav only had a couple of formal trousers, a shirt, a tie and no other choice. His throat went dry when he heard this. He felt as if his secret was out and he had been exposed in front of everyone.

He didn't want to look into anyone's eyes and turned his head so that nobody could look at his pale face. He quickly looked at Ridima, who was busy with her notes and she didn't return his look.

A question had been on his mind since last night: would he become a dark spot in her life, diminishing her beauty like those on the moon did?

He didn't know that he would get an answer so soon. It was not merely a work meeting. To him, it was the answer to the question that his conscience had demanded last night.

Vinod would not let go of a single opportunity and made offensive comments about their relationship to others. Bullying was not new to him and was a part of his life. If someone walks against the stream, it is inevitable for those who don't like it.

But Ridima became a victim of it because of him. His self-esteem went to its lowest and his self-hatred reached its peak.

There was already uncertainty about his career in his mind. His kin in Hyderabad repeatedly asked when he was joining him, but he was in a dilemma. It made him rethink what he had achieved in the last three months.

He had joined a computer institute, thinking that it would pave a path to enter the IT industry, but this looked like a distant dream now. His salary was enough to pay the restaurant bills and for the movie tickets, but he couldn't buy another pair of clothes for himself.

After careful consideration, he concluded that his dreams would never come true here. As far his goals were concerned, he had got off track and needed to return to the right track.

He liked Ridima very much; she was his motive to work, but he knew that no one could get all that he desired. Ridima was like the colours of a rainbow, whereas his life was a black hole where every colour disappeared.

He wanted to know what she thought about their relationship and whether it was worth continuing after leaving this job. But he had decided to move to Hyderabad and did not know how to sustain the relationship. He didn't even have her mobile number yet and couldn't ask for it.

The next afternoon, they were at the lunch table and he informed her that he was no longer willing to continue this teaching job and planned to go to Hyderabad. He was planning to search for a job as a software engineer. Ridima was silent and listening to him. He mustered all his courage and asked, "What do you want your life partner to be? Who will you marry?"

"I want to marry a civil servant," she responded without giving it any serious consideration.

She informed him that she had got a marriage proposal from a boy who had just become a civil servant. But his family demanded dowry, and it didn't materialize. So, she also wanted to be a civil servant and was preparing for it. This job gave her time to study and was suitable for her preparation.

"Civil servant?" he stopped his sentence without completing it. One who could not get a software engineering job couldn't even think of becoming a civil servant.

Anubhav was sad and so was Ridima, but he had got his answer. It didn't require a dictionary to understand what she meant. She was merely helping a clumsy rookie. Her mobile number was unnecessary now, and he didn't ask for it. Instead, he was grateful to her.

When they were off work in the evening, she said, "Will you drop me at my apartment, or is this it?"

"It's the last day I'll drop you at your apartment. You have to travel alone from tomorrow. And do you know one thing?" Anubhav revealed, "MH-CTC is in the opposite direction and I needed to travel back every day." He accompanied her daily to drop her off at the apartment and would then travel back. She didn't react to his revelation.

She kept quiet and didn't say anything on the way and neither did Anubhav. The auto-rickshaw reached outside her apartment building and stopped. She said, "Anubhav, wait for five minutes. I need to return your networking book."

Ridima was teaching computer networks to the students at the institute. Anubhav had his academic computer network book with him, which was not available in the library, so he had given it to her to prepare for the classes.

Soon, she came back with the book and handed it over to Anubhav.

"I know where MH-CTC is located. It's near Wanwadi Bazaar. I have been there many times," she said and then paused.

"How many secrets have you buried inside of you?" she asked, looking at his inexpressive face and she also became silent. There was no smile on her face.

He looked at her face and finally into her eyes for the last time without saying a word. There was no shine in her eyes; it felt as though there was deep, bottomless water inside them and he could see hundreds of questions floating in them. He was not prepared to answer any of them.

There were many other complex questions in his life. Before revealing any other secrets, he needed to find the answer to his questions.

He said goodbye, raising his hand halfway and her lips remained sealed. Ridima remained standing as if testing the strength of the invisible barrier between them. Their eyes expressed their feelings and there was nothing he needed to say, except to believe that when a significant dream is waiting to come true, many other dreams demand sacrifice. He would not let fate write his destiny; instead, he would write it himself.

He returned to the auto-rickshaw and asked the driver to go towards the airport instead of MH-CTC. He asked the auto driver to stop near the same broken airport boundary wall where he had not visited since joining the institute.

He climbed over the wall, looking for the flights and the little birds. The weather had swept away the leaves from the tree. The birds had deserted the nest and the trees and no chicks were in sight.

PART 3

One More Bet

13

REACHING CYBERABAD

Anubhav lived in Pune for about a year. Though he got a couple of job opportunities, the gateway to his dreams remained closed. He felt guilty residing with a relative for such a long time. He explored all possible options but none of his efforts succeeded.

Changing a place may change one's luck. Anubhav was on a train for the second time to find a job in a new city. This time, he boarded the Hussain Sagar Express to Hyderabad from Pune railway station. Though the purpose remained the same as when he had arrived in Pune last year, the journey was not as frightening or wild and not full of apprehensions.

A year of struggle and every encounter taught him exceptional lessons. Now, he was prepared, equipped and knew what he needed to do.

It was the summer of May 2004 when Anubhav arrived at Hyderabad Deccan railway station. The weather and city didn't fill him with awe like before. He was no longer an ignoramus villager who had landed in Rome.

His kin, Major Amit Kumar was posted in a major training centre, the Military College of Electrical and Mechanical Engineering, MCEME. With his dreams, Anubhav shifted to another army quarter located in Trimulgherry, another cantonment area, but this time, it was an officer's quarter in Secunderabad.

Cantonment areas had many things in common. Like Pune Cantonment, it was also vast and full of trees, greenery and many military units. There were similar playgrounds, large open areas, houses up to two stories, a temple, a gurudwara, a CSD canteen and an army hospital. It was not new to him and he no longer fantasized about it. Though the quarter was different from the previous one in Pune, there were more bedrooms, bigger gardens and more amenities.

He didn't want to waste a single day like he had passed the initial weeks in Pune. On the first day, he inspected the surroundings: the newspaper agency, internet cafe, book store and the nearest bus stand. Like every cantonment city, a local market called Lal Bazaar was near the family quarters. Lal Bazaar bus stop was just two stops from the family quarters bus stand and one could walk if there was no hurry.

He got everything he needed within walking distance. His kin had subscribed to several newspapers and magazines, including The Times of India. So he didn't need to go outside to buy a newspaper. He could read newspapers all seven days of the week. Although he needed to wait for the Times Ascent to find a job posting as it was a weekly editorial, astrology was welcome seven days a week. The internet was also more affordable here as there were many cyber cafes in the market.

His decision to leave Pune and relocate to Hyderabad seemed to be a good one. However, the memories of Ridima were still fresh in his mind.

One should never live in the past; the past is dead, and it's the haunt of the ghost. Look at tomorrow and build the castle of life on the rock of the future. Believing this to be true, he was headed that way.

There were many points of interest in Hyderabad, but he was most interested in HITECH city. The Hyderabad Information Technology and Engineering Consultancy City abbreviated as HITECH City, was located in Hyderabad in the current Telangana state, also known as Cyberabad. It was the result of the IT revolution that India had witnessed.

HITECH city was far from his place, being separated from the old part of the twin city and was about fifteen miles away from Secunderabad. There was no direct bus, so he needed to go to the central bus station near Secunderabad railway station. Buses were available to every part of the city from this point, so he caught a bus to Secunderabad railway station from there.

Once more, a new pocket diary was in his pocket. He wrote down the bus number he had boarded and noted the names and locations of all significant buildings, hotel details, etc. on the way. He was quick to prepare his new pocket map, noting the establishments alongside the road or any other sign visible from the bus.

Although it took half an hour to reach the central bus stop, he spent sufficient time learning the different bus routes, timings and their frequencies. He needed to board the bus route number 10H, starting from Secunderabad and ending at Kondapur. HITECH city was the fortieth stop after travelling for over an hour and the frequency of the bus was quite good. The first bus was ready at 7 a.m., while the last bus service was till 10 p.m. and it ran at intervals of less than twenty minutes. He boarded the bus only after recording all the necessary information in his pocketbook.

The HITECH city was visible from a distance when he reached it. Despite the fear spiralling through him, he was thrilled at his first sight of it. He got off the bus at a bus stand in the middle of IT Park. The first view was incredible, where a ten-storey cylindrical-shaped building housed IT giants such as Microsoft, IBM, Toshiba, Wipro, Oracle and many more. This centrepiece of the IT city was aptly called Cyber Towers. It offered five hundred thousand square feet of workspace.

He read all the names on the board outside it and gathered as much information as possible. Like the Cyber Towers, another huge campus named Cyber Gateway housed giants like Dell, Capitol Records and the software behemoth, Microsoft. Anubhav forgot the pain that he had gone through in Pune and once again, the same euphoria, ecstasy and joy filled him.

Though this city was as big as the IT Park in Pune, it differed in shape and architecture. But one thing was common – small tea and snack shops and stalls at every corner of the streets. He could see a similar crowd of IT professionals roaming around it for the same reasons: tea and cigarettes.

Anubhav hung around these people, trying to get their names and identify the company for which they were working. He dreamt of his future. He would be working in one of these offices, having an identity card around his neck. If the thought of working here was so fascinating, how would it feel to actually work here!

14

CONFIDENCE IS MORE THAN A STATE OF MIND

Anubhav continued his efforts in all possible ways. Like Pune, there was hardly any company he had not visited and submitted his resume once or twice. Visiting a new company and exploring any possible opportunity were the only things left in his life. There was no fun or excursions.

All new places come with new challenges and so did Hyderabad. Bogus job consultancies had trapped him in Pune, making money by taking enrolment fees from a job seeker and delivering no service. However, it was a complex business technique here. There was a more well-organized way to hire a fresh graduate looking for a job. There were hundreds of training institutes that posted advertisements in newspapers stating that multiple positions for trainee software engineers were available.

When he approached them, he found that they offered a programming course of choice of three to six months duration and charged between twenty thousand to forty thousand rupees, depending on the programming language of choice. They promised a campus placement, but they had none.

These institutes offered a letter of experience for the desired duration for an extra payment after the completion of the course. This approach was much costlier than a one-time registration charge, a thug of a different kind.

Anubhav had never thought of getting a job using a fake letter of experience and the idea didn't tempt him. He had learned to distinguish between bogus and genuine job postings by looking at the repetitions and details of advertisements. No genuine company posted job openings every week.

He also met a couple of job agents who promised a back door entry to a few well-known companies. They asked for a hefty sum between two lakh and three lakh rupees. This money was shared between the recruitment person and the job agent. He was familiar with the corruption and bribes in getting a government job, but seeing it in this sector surprised him. Both the ideas did not appeal to him, not only because they were against his principles, but also, because he couldn't afford them.

It took about two months for Anubhav to get an opportunity when he came across a recruitment drive by one of the major IT companies, Oracle Corporation. There were openings for trainee software engineers. He applied for it on its job portal.

He received the first response from an employer after applying to hundreds of companies through its career section. The recruitment drive was to be held the following weekend.

A warm feeling arose within him. Applying through a job portal had finally worked; otherwise, he had lost interest in the company website's career section. Its venue was a grand five-star hotel, the Hyderabad Marriott Hotel & Convention Centre, in the City Centre near Hussain Sagar Lake.

Anubhav reached the venue the following Saturday. He was about to attend an interview at a company like Oracle and visit a five-star hotel, so his heart was beating fast. He didn't know what a five-star hotel looked like from the inside.

It had rained the previous night and water had collected all over the street. It was still drizzling in the morning when he started, enough to moisten him. The road outside the hotel complex was busy and nobody was going on foot to the hotel; everybody was in a car there and the security person at the gate was saluting them. Anubhav understood that he would not be allowed to enter like this, so he kept the printout handy as he approached the gate.

"I am here for the Oracle recruitment drive," he declared, showing the printout to the security guard at the main gate.

"The first floor, follow the sign at the lobby," returned the gateman, looking at the call letter. There were golden signboards on the pathway saying 'Oracle Recruitment Drive' and he followed them.

Before this, he had not been to a five-star hotel and now found himself in a wonderland. As he walked through the grand porch of the hotel, he looked about distractedly and screwed up his eyes as if dazzled by the sun. The hotel porch was almost half the size of his village. It was sparkling in the light and its ceiling was very high. The door was huge.

Two sentries on both sides of the door were dressed in a traditional red uniform. He looked dumbfounded but continued moving forward. When he reached the big door, both the sentries saluted him. They were different from the guard at the main gate outside and did not question anything.

No one had ever saluted him like this before and he was about to respond likewise but his sixth sense alerted him and his right hand was arrested in his trouser pocket.

How should a man act in a five-star hotel? He did not know. He had seen such a hotel only in movies or from outside several times but had remained away from its entrance. He stopped there for a while and was still contemplating what he should do next.

A few more young men were behind him. He heaved a sigh of relief and made up his mind that all he needed to do was blindly follow them.

However, he was worried about his attire. He wasn't sure what would be appropriate for such a place. He wiped the sweat from his forehead and gently checked his hair with one hand.

As he walked inside, he was amazed. The magnificent reception lobby was crowded, although it was a planned schedule and a limited number of candidates had been invited. He stopped but his eyes scanned everything around him.

Unexpectedly, he heard a familiar voice, "Hey, Anubhav. You are also here!"

He turned back and found his classmate and friend, Narendra standing there. A couple of fellows were following him and they walked towards him. They were classmates and hugged each other. It was a welcome surprise.

He found four of his classmates and a few juniors from college who had been in Hyderabad for more than six months. They rented an apartment in Begumpet and were staying together. He took their contact numbers and addresses and wrote them in his pocket book.

Finally, he had friends with him who were in the same boat and were ready to launch their job campaign together. They had gathered all the information before Anubhav arrived and told him to follow them. They walked together to the hotel's first floor, towards a big conference room where the HR representative had invited them to meet.

The lobby was long and a soft designer rug was lying through it. The chenille of the carpet was about an inch thick. It was being pressed under the shoes of the people walking on it.

Anubhav's feet lagged behind those of the others as he found a squeaking sound following him, which was arising from his shoes. His shoes were wet as they had absorbed rainwater on the way and his socks were soaked in water.

His feelings swiftly changed from joy to deep anxiety. He maintained a suitable distance so that no one could notice it. He reached the presentation room. The corner chair in the first row was empty, and he sat on it.

Tea and coffee vending machines were placed on a stand at a corner of the room. Candidates were taking a cup of the beverage of their choice along with the cookies that were kept there. Anubhav remained seated and didn't budge from his position. The squeaking noise from his shoes still echoed in his ears and he was nervous. He wanted to prevent anyone there from noticing his shoes.

The time to wait was over and a team of two HR staff members entered the conference room and welcomed them warmly. A digital projector had already been installed and one of them connected his laptop to it. He began the company presentation and started running PowerPoint slides while the other HR representative went through it and explained each PPT slide to the candidates assembled in front of them.

She pointed first to the slides and then gave details, gazing at the candidates. She looked at the candidates sitting in the front row repeatedly, taking and answering the usual questions. It made him feel afraid, and he crossed his legs and hid his feet under the chair.

The presentation was going on and there was a moment when she turned towards him, explaining one of the presentation slides. Anubhav immediately looked down at his feet which lay one over the other. His feet were inadvertently facing the HR representative's direction and this made him sweat, and shake inwardly.

She must have seen two long tears on the bottom of his shoes and socks. His eyes clouded over with deep concern. He began tracking his footsteps on the carpet in the direction in which he had stepped.

The footmarks were visible as light mud tracks marked the shimmering maroon rug up to his seat. He forgot everything that he knew and had learned. His self-confidence instantly sank into a bottomless pit.

He wanted to get out of this room but couldn't find a way to do so. He remained seated and waited for the presentation to finish. He hated himself, thinking that everybody was looking at him as he had messed up the carpet.

He blamed himself for this situation. This situation could have been different had he not sat in the first row. He knew from school and college that a front-row seat was not for him and he always avoided it. However, he had allowed this disaster. Furthermore, it was due to his negligence that the shoes had not been repaired again.

While reproaching himself with endless thoughts of self-criticism, he found that the orientation session was over and the HR representatives required them to move to another hall to take a written test. Anubhav kept sitting till the last candidate moved out and left it before the next batch could enter. He left the hotel without appearing for the written test and interview once more.

Self-confidence is not just a state of mind and it cannot be practiced. One should have a way to procure it. At least, one should have decent attire to wear in order to appear for an interview. Your body movements as well as level of confidence are commanded by how comfortable you are.

He had only a pair of shirts and trousers and had been using the same footwear for the last four years, which had been ripped and repaired many times. It had been repaired so often that the cobbler said that it could no longer be repaired. If he had seen another cobbler, he might have fixed it. He was blaming himself for the disgraceful incident throughout the way home.

15

A CALCULATED RISK IS WORTH IT

After walking around for over two months, Anubhav had got his first chance to appear in an interview in Hyderabad. It was a disaster, but it didn't discourage him. Failure was with him like a cloud and there was nothing left to be scared of. Instead, he was happy to meet his college friends in the same city who were looking for a job like him.

Five of his college friends lived in the Begumpet area of Hyderabad: Narendra, Prashant, Sanjay, Ajay and Vinay. Ajay and Vijay were his juniors and the other three were his batch mates.

He began visiting them frequently. They had much more information about the ongoing walk-in interviews and what was happening there. He found someone with whom to discuss an upcoming interview or job posting and shared stories with them.

Coincidentally, their landlord's son had also completed engineering in the same year and had not been placed in any company. His name was Srinivas, and they used to call him Srini. Being a local, Srini understood the companies' whereabouts and had good connections. He had plenty of information that Anubhav couldn't get on his own. He wished they had met earlier.

One evening, Anubhav came to meet them at their apartment. It was not a usual gathering but there was gravity in the room as though secret preparations were underway for a robbery or looting a bank.

"Hi, dudes. How are you doing?" Anubhav broke the seriousness in the room.

"Hi, Anubhav. It's good to see you here. You came at the right time," Narendra acknowledged him and everyone in the room welcomed him.

"There is an interview planned on Monday, in two days, and we are planning to attend it," Narendra told him.

"Really? Is it a walk-in?" Anubhav asked intently.

"No, it's not an open walk-in interview. Call letters have been sent to only a few candidates," said Srinivas.

Anubhav was disheartened and said wistfully, "It means I can't go." He sat on one side of the bed.

This multipurpose bed at the central upper side was a study table, a meeting table for discussion, a dining table during lunch and dinner and a deck to play rummy in free time. The good thing about this bed was that it belonged to Narendra, and he liked cleanliness. The room was cleaned every morning, and the bedsheet was changed weekly, unlike any other room in the apartment.

"Brother, why are you worried? You are not the only one. None of us got the call letter." Srinivas was relaxed and positive.

"What do you mean then? What are you guys preparing for?"

"No, we are going to the same place, Four Soft. We will get the call letters," said the other two boys.

"How will you get it, buddy?" Anubhav asked him curiously.

Srinivas continued, "There is nothing to worry about; one of my friends has got the call letter."

Then, he pointed his finger towards Prashant who was sitting at the computer table and doing something.

Srinivas explained, "Prashant is not playing any Mario on the computer. He is preparing call letters for us."

"How come?" Anubhav exclaimed, and the mystery deepened for him.

"I have forwarded him my friend's call letter." Srini explained the trick, laughing and patting Anubhav's shoulder. "He is editing it for every one of us. He needs to replace the name and email address of the recipient and the call letter will be ready. Isn't that easy?"

Anubhav was a naive boy, and he never told a lie.

He was uncomfortable with this idea and asked, "Are you guys cheating?"

Anubhav was reluctant to give his assent to this and was afraid of the consequences. "What if we are caught?" he asked, almost trembling.

"It's not anything new. We do it every time," said Narendra, taking Anubhav by surprise, who had never imagined opening the door to destiny like this.

Anubhav went towards the computer table and looked at what Prashant was doing on the computer.

"Dude, can I see the original call letter?"

Prashant opened the mailbox and showed it to him saying, "Look at it."

These fellows were experts in forging interview call letters. This trick worked for them; they had attended many interviews, almost twice a month as opposed to Anubhav, who had waited six months to get into one.

Anubhav was optimistic about the idea and found it helpful.

"Oh, yeah... create it for me as well."

Shortly, the call letters were ready for everybody in the room. All that was needed now was to take a printout and plan to go to HITECH city. Prashant copied the edited call letters into a pen drive.

"Guys, let's go now. It is Saturday today. Sri Laxmi Internet café will close early," said Prashant wanting to rush down to a cyber cafe.

"Let's move," Narendra said to them and was anxious to leave. "My head is feeling heavy without tea."

Sri Laxmi Cyber Café provided the cheapest internet and printouts in the area, so it was their favourite. The internet was not as easily available in those days as it is today; there were no smartphones and mobile services were limited to calls and texts. Students and the common public depended on cyber cafes for internet use, checking their email and taking printouts.

Anubhav and the others were excited and came out of the apartment. They started walking on the street towards Sri Laxmi Cyber Café.

He was happy that his visit to his friends had been worth it and he would be able to attempt an interview tomorrow because of them. However, he was nervous about forging a call letter and there was a flicker of doubt in his eyes.

"Friends, isn't this like deceiving someone?" he raised his concern again.

"Who are we deceiving?" Srinivas reacted sharply.

"They are not fair in their selection process which is not based on merit. The companies invite only a limited number of candidates. There are no fair rules for short-listing a resume. They are simply calling on the basis of some reference," Srinivas complained about the recruitment process. "You will get a call if you know someone in the company. Otherwise, nobody will entertain you."

"That's true, but what if we get caught?" Anubhav wanted to prepare for any unpleasant or embarrassing situation and know the consequences if this turned out to be a misadventure.

"They are not going to call the police, are they?" he shared his fear.

"You are overthinking it," said Srinivas. "Just walk, it's easy."

"It's not deceiving anybody. We are not harming any business or going to cause any loss to anybody. The company needs some candidates and we are trying to put forward our candidature. That's it," Narendra intervened.

"It's called taking a risk, and that's what we are going to do," Prashant also shared his views.

"Did anyone catch us when we went for Oracle's interview?" said Ajay, referring to the last experience.

"Oh, my God! You guys did not get a call letter for that too?" exclaimed Anubhav. He hadn't known this before but recalled that nobody there had requested him to show the call letter, except the security guard at the main gate.

The word 'risk' mentioned by Prashant was stuck in Anubhav's mind. He needed to improve his understanding of a lie. It was a risk.

Soon, they reached Sri Laxmi Cyber Cafe. Prashant took the pen drive out of his pocket, handed it to the operator running the café and requested the printouts. The call letter was ready for everyone for five rupees each.

Everyone checked their respective call letters to ensure that their names and email IDs were correct. The group went to a nearby snack corner and ordered idlis, dosas and Irani tea. The tea sellers were famous for the Irani tea, which had originated here.

The plan had been executed and now they needed to prepare for the interview, so they said goodbye to each other and left for their apartment. Anubhav promised to meet them again on Monday at 10 a.m. near the company's office in the middle of HITECH city. Then, he walked across the street to the nearest bus stop. He needed to board the 24B bus route to Lal Bazaar. It was Monday, the day to test his knowledge and strength to face the risk. Anubhav was ready for it. He was the first to reach HITECH city.

He didn't have to wait too long as everyone was on time. At about ten, he saw his friends getting off a bus.

They assembled at the bus stop, held hands together and encouraged each other to be confident and behave as though they had an original call letter. With a thumbs-up signal, the group moved together towards the main entrance and security gate of the Cyber Tower IT Park. The Four Soft office was located on the fifth floor of the Cyber Tower.

"We have come for the interview," said Srinivas. He took out his call letter from his backpack and presented it to the security guard standing at the gate.

"Which company?" questioned the security guard.

"Four Soft Private Limited," they said together.

The guard walked towards the window of the security room inside the gate and reported to his supervisor, "Sir, a few candidates are here for the interview."

After a few minutes, the supervisor checked the record with him and replied, "There is no information on the board. No notice has been published for an interview from any company today."

"Which company do you guys need to go to?" the supervisor questioned further.

All of them handed over their call letters to him.

Companies needed to post the list of candidates coming for interviews on the board so that they could get a gate pass and enter the building.

The security guard called the central security office, which was in the main lobby of the building on the first floor.

"Sir, there are a few candidates here who have been called for an interview with Four Soft, but I have not received any notification from the company's HR department."

It took some time to clear the miscommunication. Still, everybody was allowed to go through the security gate outside the building and meet the security in-charge in the central lobby inside the main building.

The first obstacle had been cleared, and they had managed to enter the big building. All six of them reached the lobby of the building where visitor passes needed to be issued. They showed their call letters at the counter.

"Who called you?" the security person at the counter asked them. "Do you have the contact details of the HR representative?"

"Rosy Jain," Narendra replied.

"Which company?" he asked further.

"Four Soft. It is 5555," said Srini, pointing it out to him on the call letter.

The security officer took the call letter from his hand and dialled the number mentioned in it.

"Madam, we have a few candidates waiting in the lobby," he notified her.

"Interview! Is it today?" exclaimed Rosy from the other end of the call. She appeared to be confused by this.

"But, I have not called any candidates today," said Rosy.

"They have a call letter from you," clarified the security officer.

It took some time and there was confusion for a moment.

"Issue them the visitors' cards and allow them to come to my office."

The security person asked them for their photo identification. They handed over their identity cards and driving licenses and were issued a visitor pass each.

"Go to lift seven," instructed the security officer and permitted them to go to the office of Four Soft. "Don't forget to return the visitor pass before you leave," he further instructed.

The idea had worked well. "Was that not easy?" asked Srini mockingly. "That is the only need for a call letter."

Lowering his eyes, Anubhav conceded defeat as they had reached the door of the company's office.

They reached the company's reception area and informed the receptionist that they were there for the interview.

"Which HR staff member do you need to meet, sir?" the receptionist inquired.

"Rosy Jain," answered Narendra.

"Please wait, let me call her," she requested and dialled the HR room to inform her about the candidates for the interview.

In less than five minutes, a lady of average height but fairer and prettier than average came to the reception area and asked the receptionist, "Who has come for the interview?"

The receptionist turned her head and pointed to the six of them standing in the nearby waiting area.

"Hi, I am Rosy. Are you guys here for the interview?" she asked them.

"Yes, madam," everybody replied together. "We have come for the interview."

"Can I see the call letter?"

The guys handed over the printouts that were already in their hands. She looked at them. They were from the recruitment team and today's date was printed on them. Rosy thought for a while and seemed surprised.

"But I haven't issued any call letters for today. Let me check with other HR staff members if anyone has sent them." Saying so, she went back to the HR room, taking the printouts with her.

She checked with other HR staff members and found that no one had called any candidate today. She carefully checked the call letters again; it was her recruitment email id, and the emails had been sent to them about two weeks back. She was concerned because it looked like she had missed something. She logged on to her desktop and checked her mailbox.

She searched for all the six names but couldn't find any of them in her sent folder or any documents. Something was wrong.

She returned to the reception. All of them were sitting on the sofa and stood up as she approached them.

"I have not scheduled any interviews for today or sent any call letters for today's date," Rosy maintained and was perplexed. "When did you get this?"

The fellows replied promptly, "Last week." Vinay was leading the explanation this time.

"I was in Jabalpur when I received this email. I travelled and reached here last night to attend the interview only," he said and added, "I have the train ticket with me."

Coincidentally, Vinay had travelled from Jabalpur, his native place, the previous night only and the train ticket was still in his pocket. He was wearing the same trousers. He took out the train ticket and gave it to her, thinking this would support their claim.

Her tone changed instantly after hearing this and her face seemed puzzled and then looked fierce.

"Jabalpur!" she exclaimed. She further interrogated, "Are all of you from Jabalpur?"

"Yes, Madam. We are from Jabalpur," they replied in chorus.

"Oh... I am getting it now," she said a little loudly. "Tell me, from where did you get this call letter?"

Vinay's missile didn't only miss the target but rebounded on them.

"We had applied online, and we received an email last week, madam," said Vinay.

Rosy looked at all of them. They looked pitiful but were not yet willing to quit.

"We have received it, madam. Any other HR staff member may have sent it," Srinivas was leading the conversation.

"No, nobody has sent it. I have already verified it with the others," she softened, looking at their gloomy faces but at the same time, she was curious to know how they had arranged it. She said, "You guys ought to tell me the truth. How did you get it?"

"We have got it, madam," a couple of them said together, but this time, their spirits fumbled.

"Look, I am from Jabalpur. I know the boys from Jabalpur very well. They are very clever," she said, smirking a little. "You guys need to tell me, what did you do?"

Her smile gave them a little encouragement but nobody spoke this time. Everybody was looking at each other. Anubhav was hiding behind the others and could not be clearly seen.

"If you received this email, you should have it in your mailbox. Can you show it to me? Come with me to my desk and log in to your email," she commanded. She was not ready to give up and wanted to nail the irregularity.

Nobody moved as the trick had bombed horribly and they were trapped. Their faces were downcast but more than that, they were frightened and looked disappointed and hopeless. The intelligent lady assessed the situation and tried to make them feel comfortable.

"Look, I sent the call letters two weeks back and there was an interview scheduled for today. But later, I rescheduled the interview, which will now be held on next Monday, not today," she said. "I have sent the revised schedule to everyone. If you have received the first email, you must also have received the second email and updated schedule."

On hearing this, the boys understood what had gone wrong. The plan had worked fine, but they landed up on the wrong date. This blunder would not have happened if they had any clue that the interview had been postponed by a week. They had been caught red-handed and Rosy was not ready to let the matter go.

There was apprehension on everyone's faces but this was Anubhav's first experience of using a bogus call letter. He hid behind them like a fool, thinking that he shouldn't have joined them. He was extremely scared and there was no way to escape. But there was one boy who had not surrendered and still had hope.

"Didi, please excuse us. We will tell you the truth," Narendra confessed. There was a striking change in his language and he spoke as though she was no longer a stranger to him.

"Didi! Hmm..." she exclaimed and sat down on the sofa.

"Sit down, my dear brothers," she said in the same vein, making them feel comfortable. "Why are you standing?"

"Relax, drink some water and then tell me what you guys did?" She was calm this time.

"Didi, we have completed our engineering from Jabalpur this year from a college that does not have a high ranking. There was no campus placement. We have come to Hyderabad to look for a job," Narendra explained.

"I can understand that, but how did you get the call letter?" she questioned again.

"We roamed a lot and applied for many job postings, but we were not getting any response. We don't know anyone in any of the companies and we don't have any references. Every company asks for references. So, if any of us or any other friend receives a call letter, we use that to get information, edit the name and email and prepare a call letter for ourselves," said Narendra.

"By doing this, we can come inside a building and attend interviews. That is the only purpose of it and we don't have any other intentions. The call letter was to bypass the security at the gate," Prashant spilled the beans and explained the situation.

They revealed the truth. "Didi, we have come from far away. We don't know anyone here. Please guide us," Ajay added, as the tension gradually eased.

"This is not appropriate. You should not follow such a practice," the HR member cautioned them. "All of you are qualified, so, opportunities will come to you," she motivated them.

"Please let us know when the next interview will be conducted. We will follow your advice, didi."

"Didi! Hmm..." she exclaimed, laughing again.

She became silent and looked a little thoughtful now. There was no substantial reason not to allow them to take a test the following Monday, which she had scheduled.

"Let me check with my manager if he can do something for you," she said and returned to the HR room, ordering them to wait.

She went to the HR room and discussed how a few job aspirants had come to the office to attend an interview. The company was looking for freshers in good numbers, so the manager gave them an opportunity.

The mood outside was not so tense now; the fear of being caught was over but everyone looked undecided and embarrassed. Everybody was silent, not speaking to each other and anxiously waiting for Rosy to return. Everyone's eyes were pinned at the door from where she had gone inside. Every time the door opened, they stood up and then, sat down again, seeing it was not Rosy, but someone else.

"Sir, there is a break room next door. You can stop by and have some coffee or tea if you like," said the receptionist sitting there, who had been following the episode. She pointed her finger towards the break room next to the waiting area.

"No, madam, we are good," they said together. "Thank you."

But someone said, "May I have a glass of water, please?"

"Yes, of course. It's in the same area," the receptionist directed. "Right beside the coffee maker."

Everyone went to the break room. It provided the lads with some relief.

"Let's go now. We have got a chance to leave," said Ajay.

"What had to happen has happened now. Let's wait for the HR representative. She might issue a call letter for the next week. Then we will not need to fake it again," said Srini and everyone agreed.

Soon, Rosy came out of the room, carrying a register with her and asked them to make an entry. They didn't understand why she was asking for it, but they didn't have any choice.

"Come with me," she said and moved towards the door and punched her identity card on the card reader. The door opened, and she held it until everyone was inside the room. Anubhav and his friends were still wondering about what was going to happen next.

She led them into a big room with many empty cubicles around. Two other HR staff members were already present, and they had a set of question papers with them. She asked them to sit down and explained the interview process. There were multiple rounds, first a written one and then, a few technical rounds, followed by the HR interview, if one qualified for all of them.

After this, she left the room, handing over the charge to Anand and Tejal, the other HR staff members who were there to complete their first screening round – a written test.

Although their trick to forge a call letter had failed and had been a disaster this time, all of them had got an interview opportunity. The HR team had been kind enough to ignore it this time. They completed the first round which was the written test and were asked to report back at 4 o'clock for the result.

It was not yet 4 o'clock. The boys were waiting anxiously outside the lobby when Rosy joined them again, carrying a paper.

"Who is Narendra?"

"Yes, madam," Narendra raised his hand.

"And Anubhav," she announced the next qualifier.

"It's me," Anubhav raised his hand instantly.

"Both of you have qualified for the next round. You need to come for the next interview round on next Monday," she explained the remaining process.

"Sorry to the others, you have not qualified for the next round," she stated, returning to her office, "but you can apply again after six months."

Though everyone couldn't make it, all of them were happy about how it had ended.

They walked out of the Cyber Tower IT Park and straight to the nearest bus stand. All of them needed to catch the same bus except Anubhav, who had to wait longer because the bus 10H, which he needed to board, had comparatively less frequency. He remained sitting at the bus stop, staring at the tall tower, after his friends had boarded the bus to Begumpet.

Anubhav could now imagine more realistically how life would be after joining an IT company. It seemed as though he had been watching a silent movie in black and white till now. It was time to add colours to the colourless picture he had in mind.

He became so deeply lost in the swirl of dreams and feelings while looking at the tall IT building and professionals around, that he didn't realize that many of the buses that he had been waiting for passed him by.

The following Monday was going to be a big day for Anubhav. He didn't understand whether it was destiny or his courageous decision to join his friends that had made it possible. Anubhav spent the days reading books and preparing for the interview and he was ready to face the next round of challenges. Anubhav woke up early in the morning. First, he had a bath and then, he shaved and massaged his face. He washed it many times until it glowed.

After getting ready, he read the newspaper, not to check a job posting, but to know what the stars foretold him.

'Daily Horoscope, Cancer: Today, you are blessed with the moon; the sun is standing at the same position; destiny may be with you and you may expect a good gain in your past investment. You may be able to escape the messy situation you had in the past and things will be under control. You may work with great patience. You may get some incentives in terms of rewards.'

It was precisely in line with what had been happening with him since last week.

"How accurate it is! Last week was so messy. Everything that is written here happened last week. The stars are with me," Anubhav mumbled.

Anubhav's faith in astrology was strengthened. That the stars controlled destiny was beyond doubt to him. Today's prediction was encouraging and he could feel it within him. After reading this, he was sure he would win the game.

The HR staff member had asked them to come by 11 a.m. Narendra had promised to meet him there, so he needed to leave.

Narendra was also punctual and both of them reached the reception of Four Soft Private Limited at the right time.

"Good morning, madam. We have an interview scheduled for today," said Narendra at the reception. "We took the written test last week."

"Yes, I remember it. Let me inform Rosy. You can have a seat."

It took some time before Rosy entertained them and they were keenly waiting to meet her. She entered the reception area more than an hour after they arrived, but she was not looking stern like last time.

"Good morning, madam," both of them greeted her, standing up from the sofa.

"Good morning to both of you," the HR member replied as she approached them.

"We can't proceed with your candidature at this time," Rosy said. "I am sorry to say this."

They were confused, and it left a frown on their faces. "Why, madam?" Narendra asked her. "May we know what has gone wrong?"

"Our senior management is unconvinced regarding how you forged the call letter. It comes under unethical practice and can't be encouraged, so the management has decided not to consider your candidature this time," she said, explaining the reason behind it.

"We apologize for doing so," Anubhav said apologetically.

"Don't be disappointed. You guys have the ability and a perfect academic background," she reassured them. "You will get opportunities very soon."

"Best of luck to both of you," she said as she walked towards the door.

Both of them were dejected as they couldn't believe this would happen after qualifying for one round. The meeting was over in less than five minutes.

Do the stars really drive someone's destiny or is it just a belief? Anubhav was back at home, but a stream of questions flowed through his mind. He wondered if it was correct that whatever happened to you had been written already.

The horoscope had predicted a favourable week for him. He looked for the newspaper and went through the sixth page again that had the horoscope predictions and read it carefully for every prediction of all the twelve zodiac signs.

He discovered that it was merely a universal positive thought that could be related to the daily life events of anyone. The human brain is very agile and connects these predictions to the self. It is not the power of the stars but your decisiveness, ability and willingness to take risks that decide your future.

PART 4

The Depths of Despair

16

LIFE IS PRICELESS

When one faces successive failures, the shadow of disappointment takes control. Anubhav did his best to get a job but luck was not on his side.

His hopes sank gradually and then, something transpired that dashed all his hopes at once. His kin had been posted there for a year of training which was about to be completed. He received the orders for his new posting and needed to move to another city in a month.

It necessitated that Anubhav look for another place to live.

He was still unemployed and getting accommodation without making any money was unthinkable. His dreams were on the verge of being shattered and it became tough to stay optimistic and keep up the resilience that he had initially displayed.

Everyone does not have the right to dream except those who can afford it. Hopelessness surrounded Anubhav from all sides. He decided that his life was a burden on this earth that must be lifted off it. The thought of committing suicide started taking root in his mind.

He lost interest in job postings and interviews and started looking at ways to end his life. Suicide was an act of a loser and no person who committed suicide was a subject of admiration. He would remain an object of pity for a few days after his death and then be forgotten forever. He didn't want the world to know about his cowardice, so he began looking for a way and an idea through which no one could ever know that he had killed himself. He started looking for a possible way that could be related to any significant accident, rather than an apparent suicide situation.

The editorial of job postings was no longer of any interest to him but a page with news about any train or road accidents, medical negligence, clinical trials or any other unnatural death was his focus now.

At first, he thought of jumping in front of a moving truck or heavy vehicle. However, this was accompanied by a risk of survival and there was a chance of breaking his bones and becoming handicapped forever. That would be even worse. Instead of removing the burden, Anubhav could become a permanent burden. Meeting with a road accident was not a sensible choice. It was not always fatal, so he needed to plan something different.

The swine flu pandemic was a human respiratory infection caused by an influenza virus that spread through the death of pigs due to one of its strains. It was a deadly disease and there was limited vaccine available for it. Scientists worldwide were looking for more vaccines and human trials were going on. There was at least one article every day about such a clinical trial in the new editorial that he was reading.

Anubhav found a few interesting stories in the newspaper about the volunteers participating in the swine flu vaccine clinical trials. They were interviewed and their photos were published in newspapers and magazines. It occurred to him to participate in such a clinical trial. Though these were safe and had not caused any death so far and his purpose would remain incomplete, he had an opportunity to make his life worthwhile to others. The volunteers were usually older than him and he was sure that he could represent his age group.

He fantasized that this might shine a spotlight on him so that his name may become recognized, which could help him get a job. If the trial fails and the person dies, there must be some compensation for his family. Dying for such a cause would not only help his family but humanity as well.

Osmania Medical College was one of the top medical schools in the subcontinent. The doctors and scientists in its research centre were involved in research and analysis. He decided to go to this institute the next day and inquire if there was any vaccine and clinical trial going on. He wanted to volunteer for such a clinical trial.

Staying up all night was not new to him but for the first time, his mind was full of frightening thoughts of what would happen once he died and how life would be after death. Would he go to hell for committing suicide? What would happen to his family?

The chorus of birds singing outside started at dawn and the sun was about to rise. But he was still thinking and trying to get some sleep. He felt despair at his ultimate fate. Although his dreams were broken and the sunrise meant nothing to him, it was time to get ready. He got up from the bed and got ready to go to Osmania Medical College.

The college was one of the oldest medical colleges in the country, established in 1846 during the British era. It was the only institute of its kind in the state and a large crowd visited the hospital every day. People from all over the state and with every disease could be seen there.

A couple of security guards were outside the hospital entrance but were not checking anyone. Anubhav had no idea of any department, so he walked towards the security cabin. Before he could ask him any question, the security guard questioned aloud, "What happened to you? Which department do you want to go to?"

"Fever, it seems like swine flu..." said Anubhav.

"Go straight to the second building. It's on the second floor," said the guard, guiding Anubhav, using his finger.

His solemn eyes roved around while his feet kept moving towards the treatment centre. If one needed to see suffering, such a hospital was the right place for it.

"Which doctor do you need to go to?" the staff nurse at the counter asked him before he could open his mouth.

"No, I am not a patient. I have heard that the doctors are researching a swine flu vaccine and looking for volunteers to participate in the clinical research trials," he said. "I am willing to volunteer."

Hearing this, the nurse gawked at him for a while and said, "This is the OPD. We enroll and examine patients here. I don't know anything about this, but Dr. Sridhar Reddy will be able to tell you." Saying that, she called the attendant and asked him to take Anubhav to the doctor's office.

"Thank you, madam. Have a good day," Anubhav said to her and walked away with the office attendant to the first floor below.

There were many nameplates with the name of the doctors and their specialties. He saw a nameplate stating 'Dr. Sridhar Reddy', who was the head of the Virology Department of the medical institute, on the door of a big room. The attendant asked him to wait outside and went inside the room to inform doctor about him.

The doctor was surprised to know that a young boy was looking for him and wanted to participate in a clinical trial. After a brief interval, the doctor called and asked him, "Why do you want to participate in a clinical trial?"

"For the society. I want to make my society immune to this disease."

He tried his best to impress the doctor. Dr. Reddy listened to him carefully and asked all the relevant questions. He said, "Medical trials are a long and complex process. There is a complex legal procedure to go through. We don't have such a facility, though we do some trials on patients to collect data. But these are pre-approved methods and are limited to hospital patients," said Dr. Reddy. "I appreciate your vision and passion for working for society, but you are not in the right place."

The idea of a clinical trial had failed, so he had only the first two options left: death on the road or a train accident. He was baffled about what to do next.

He boarded a different bus. The quarters were about a mile from the nearest bus stop where he got off the bus on this route. Many street vendors and taxi drivers were living alongside this road. It was a deserted street with trees and bushes and was connected to a narrow trail that was a shortcut to the family quarters.

Everything was as usual till he reached the midway of the trail. As he walked towards the middle of the path, he saw a bustle like never before and his blood ran cold.

The body of a man about forty years old was hanging from a tree. It was hardly twenty feet away at the left side of the trail on which he was walking. A group of ten to twenty people had surrounded the tree. It was an apparent suicide. Anubhav stopped in his tracks.

At first, he decided to move on. It was not only disturbing, but also, a troubling scene. But thinking about his idea of suicide, he couldn't move any further. He turned left and joined the crowd.

"What happened?" he questioned a man standing next to him. "Who is this person?"

"This man hanged himself from this tree."

"Oh, sorry to hear this, but why?" Anubhav continued questioning.

"He couldn't repay his loan. The bank seized his taxi last month."

Anubhav had seen this person several times driving his taxi. The cab was parked near a slum house nearby, by the street.

"It's a white Toyota Corolla," he said and added, "I have seen him driving it."

The police were about to reach. No one dared to bring the body down. Anubhav left the place to avoid being interrogated.

Around 6 p.m., he reached the quarter. He narrated this story to his kin and a couple of his friends. It didn't disturb them like him. They asked a few questions which he couldn't answer and then, became busy talking to each other as if nothing had happened. But Anubhav's mind was agitated. The terrifying scene of the body hanging from a tree couldn't leave his mind for a second.

What was going to happen next? What would happen to the deceased's family after him? His mind started asking these tough questions, and he wanted to know what would happen to life after death.

The evening tea and snacks were ready, but he could not eat or drink anything. He decided to visit the house of this taxi driver and started back towards the slum, taking the same route he had taken sometime back.

His feet were moving faster than usual and he was breathing hard. He reached the place where he had seen the car parked the last time. By then, it was sunset, and the twilight had just started.

He heard a couple of women and men mourning loudly and he followed the painful cries. A light bulb was hanging on a small pole in the front space of the slum house of the family. People were gathering around it. He tried to breathe normally.

Anubhav didn't know anyone there. Most of the housemaids working for the officers' families lived in this slum area and he knew a few of them. His gaze passed over the faces in the crowd in the courtyard of the house. He tried to look for a familiar face but couldn't identify anyone. He stood there for about half an hour, observing the scene around him.

The mourning was unbearable, and he wanted to observe the family closely. He started moving around in the crowd and reached the front.

The man's dead body was lying on a grass mat on the ground and the shroud was yet to be arranged. Eight to ten women were wailing and he could quickly identify the dead man's wife among them. She was wailing, her voice was choked, and she was losing consciousness.

Two women held her, trying to keep her clothes in order and sprinkled water on her face. An older woman was with her, trying to hold her tightly and weeping simultaneously. She was the dead man's mother and looked stronger than his wife.

At this time, a toddler who was about two years old and seemed to be his younger son, crawled towards his father's dead body and sat on his chest, patting his face and chest.

"Papa is dead," said an older boy, who approached the toddler and pulled his younger brother off the dead body. He was about seven to eight years old and probably knew what death meant.

Anubhav was watching everything closely. The little boy thought his father would wake up and hold him in his arms like before. The older son was also unaware of death precisely, but he heard people saying that his father had died. He was looking at the people around in surprise, thinking about why the crowd had gathered at his house and was continuously holding his younger brother.

Anubhav moved closer to the family and looked at the old father, who had hardly any flesh on his body. The older man looked into his eyes as if to call him. Anubhav approached and sat on the ground next to him. The older man who was crying fell into his arms. He shared his misfortune with Anubhav, "My son is dead. The bank agents took his taxi with them. I asked him to go back to our village. We have a piece of land to farm and we can survive. But he disagreed and wanted to send his two sons to a private school in the city. He wanted to give them the best education. Everything is finished. I have lost my son."

Anubhav had not seen him before, nor did the man know who Anubhav was, but he was looking for a shoulder on which he could cry.

Anubhav was speechless. Despite his sorrow for the family, he was unable to reciprocate. His mind, which had never been without a web of thoughts for a single moment, was now numb.

"How can I help you when I don't know how to help myself?" he wanted to say to the old man but kept his words to himself. His eyes welled up with tears and he wanted to cry with him too but couldn't do it in a crowd of unfamiliar people.

He would surely cry if he stayed here any longer, so he decided to leave the place and return. He had received the answers to all the questions running through his mind for about a month at this place.

He had seen death from so close for the first time in his life. He was full of grief and his eyes started shedding tears while he was walking back. He wanted to cry his heart out, but he didn't want to be seen by anyone. One thought was racing in his mind continuously and now came to his lips, 'Would it be the same scene at my home if I commit suicide?'

Anubhav was halfway through to the quarter. It was a deserted area with trees and bushes on both sides of the street. He glanced along the trail; nobody could be seen and no one could hear him at this place.

Anubhav could no longer stop himself and burst into tears. He walked over the trail and sat on the ground, pushing the bushes aside and going further in. A loud cry echoed through the darkness, a raw and anguished symphony resonating with unbearable pain.

He had suppressed it in his heart for a long time and it was time to let it out. He cried out as loud as he could, hiding in the middle of the bushes. There was no one to listen to him.

"I will never think of committing suicide again, whatever the circumstances," Anubhav cried, looking at the stars above in the sky. It was a commitment made to himself under the dark sky in the presence of twinkling stars. He had understood how priceless life was. Death does not have the solution to any problem but life does. Only life allows us to address every situation.

17

ALWAYS ANOTHER WAY

This most unfortunate episode of an unknown taxi driver engrossed Anubhav in beliefs that were no less than enlightenment. He developed a strong understanding of physical and mental health. He was more mindful of his physical, mental and emotional condition than ever.

He could not see the path ahead with great clarity but he understood that he needed a great deal of mental and physical nourishment and continuous learning. Every struggle gave him new wisdom. The taxi driver's death was like a compass to envision the path ahead.

Anubhav's mind was preparing for battle once again. But there was not enough time left. His kin was about to move to a different city in another state in the next fifteen days, which meant that he would need a new place to live if he wanted to stay in Hyderabad and search for a job.

It was morning and his kin was getting ready to go to the office. He asked, "Anubhav, what are you going to do next? Have you planned anything?"

"I have a couple of friends living in Begumpet. I will shift in with them for a couple of months," Anubhav replied promptly, as he had prepared his reply already.

"I am waiting for a couple of interview results and expect to get an offer soon," he declared.

In reality, he had no clue as to what to do and where to live after a fortnight. If he could not arrange something for himself, he would have no choice but to go back to his village. He knew his dreams would be over if he returned to the village. There were no means of communication, no newspaper and no internet. His future was decided there: farm labour and cattle feeding.

He would have to take any job providing shelter and food in the next fifteen days. Once this happened, he was prepared to rewrite his dreams from the beginning. He wanted to stay in Hyderabad, so he required a job to survive.

Without wasting a day, Anubhav started visiting restaurants and housing societies, looking for any job as a housekeeper, security guard, waiter or whatever was available.

Anubhav passed through a nearby tea corner when he saw a familiar face with tea and buns in his hand. There was a housing society called Laxmi Park Co-operative Housing Society next to the family quarters. He had seen this older man of about seventy years working as a watchman there. He might be able to help, Anubhav realized.

"Good morning, sir!" Anubhav stopped by the tea stall.

"Good morning, my son! How are you doing today?"

"One cup of tea," Anubhav ordered first and then responded to the old man.

"Are you the one who looks after Laxmi Park Housing Society?"

"Yes."

"You work very hard. I see you 24/7," said Anubhav, admiring him.

"Yes. It has been many months since I have been asking for one more person," answered the old man. "But the chairman always tells me to look for an honest person who can do the job."

Listening to this, Anubhav felt that luck was possibly on his side. "I am looking for a job. Can I join you?"

"But you seem to be educated," the old man was surprised. "This job is not for a degree holder."

"I need a job urgently. I have graduated, so I can do much more than watch a building. I can handle society work like accounting and any other work that requires literacy." He desperately tried to convince him. For a minute, he became silent.

His eyes constantly looked at the older man's face and said millions of words. While he remained calm, the tears were about to fall from his eyes. The older man read the honesty in his face and his solemn voice touched his heart. It didn't take any effort for the man to understand that the young boy was down and out.

"I would be happy," the old man responded positively. "I will talk to the society chairman and recommend you to work with me."

"You need to come before 9 a.m.," he instructed further. "Otherwise, the chairman will leave for work and return only by 6 p.m.."

"Thank you very much! I will be there by 8 a.m.," Anubhav was delighted.

By then, both had finished the tea.

"How much is the bill for both of us?" Anubhav asked the tea seller promptly.

"Ten rupees for two cups of tea and five rupees for a bun," the tea seller calculated and told him.

"Are you paying for me as well?" the man questioned eagerly.

"Yes, I will be happy to pay for you."

Anubhav took the money from his pocket and gave it to the tea seller. It was a little bribe that he could afford.

"Thank you, dear," said the old man. "See you tomorrow." He was pleased and waved his hand as he left the place.

Anubhav was happy after a long time. It gave him hope that kept his dreams alive. It came when he had only three days left before his kin had to move to another city.

Although the older man looked satisfied and required a partner, Anubhav had reason to worry. He couldn't speak Telugu, the local language. Many other societies sought a local candidate who could talk in Telugu and understand the local language.

This concern didn't let him sleep at night and he was prepared to meet the challenge and planned to learn the language within a month, but decided that he would plead for the job. He must get it at any cost.

It was 7:30 in the morning and he reached the Laxmi Co-operative Housing Society. Near the main gate, he found the same older man washing the cars parked in the society parking lot.

"Good morning, sir!"

"Good morning, young man," replied the older man while washing a car. "You are on time. Let's go and meet the society chairman before he leaves for his office."

He stopped washing the car and asked Anubhav to follow him. They walked to the second floor of the adjacent building where Mr. Lakshman Rao, the society chairman's flat was located. He rang the bell, and the door opened. It was his housemaid who opened the door.

"Is Mr. Rao at home? He had called me in the morning."

"He is here, getting ready for office," the maid responded.

"Come inside, Fauji. Just give me two minutes."

Mr. Rao recognized who it was at the gate and spoke loudly from the adjacent room, listening to the conversation at the main door.

The older man entered the living room and Anubhav followed him and stood near the door but inside the room. Soon, Mr. Rao joined them.

"Good morning, sir."

"Good morning, Fauji. Is this the boy you talked about yesterday?"

"Yes, sir. This is the same boy," the old man pointed his hand toward Anubhav.

"What is your name, young man?" Mr. Rao asked. "Have you gone to school?"

"Sir, I am Anubhav and I have graduated."

"That is good, but I need a watchman who would look after the society," Mr. Rao said.

"I understand, sir. I would be happy to take what you pay for a watchman," Anubhav acknowledged politely and didn't look for any negotiation.

"You will get five thousand rupees a month and a Diwali bonus of one month's salary once you have completed a year. We have a servants' quarter in the society office and you must be available anytime, 24x7, if you choose to live there," Mr. Rao explained.

"I need it. I am good at working 24x7."

"Fauji, take the police verification form from the society office, complete it and he can work with you," Mr. Rao instructed the older man. Mr. Reddy was the society secretary.

"Thank you, sir," Anubhav showed his gratitude and both of them left Mr. Rao's house. Anubhav was surprised that he didn't ask if he knew Telugu, unlike any other society chairman or secretary he had encountered before.

"Doesn't he need a Telugu-speaking person?" asked Anubhav, while walking down the stairs. "I don't know Telugu and was worried about it."

Fauji laughed and said, "This society is full of army personnel and everybody can speak Hindi in this society," Fauji clarified his doubt.

"I was a soldier in the Indian army and was posted here when I retired. I settled here after my retirement," said the man.

Anubhav understood the reason behind his nickname, Fauji. The older man was a retired veteran and had looked after this society for more than thirty years after his retirement. He had a house nearby and lived with his wife and a grandson. His son had died in a road accident.

Fauji showed him the servant's room just near the entrance. It was for society guards who could be there 24/7. It was a small room of ten by ten square feet. There was a cot inside it and a kerosene stove in one corner with some utensils lying near it.

"You can stay here," Fauji showed the small room to Anubhav.

"If you want, you can make extra money by washing these cars. I get one hundred rupees a month from each car owner, but I have a condition for it," said Fauji, returning to the car he had left washing.

What else did the poor boy need? It was a monthly bonus for him.

"What do I need to do?"

"I will keep collecting the payment from the owners and give you half the money for a car wash. There are ten cars and we can make five hundred rupees each."

"Of course I will."

"Remember that this is the first job you should do early in the morning. The car owners start going to the office at around 7 a.m., so the cars should dry before they are needed," Fauji completed the terms and conditions.

"I will," said the boy, accepting all the conditions without any negotiations or questions.

Anubhav was happy after a long period of turmoil in his mind. Getting a job was not as difficult as he had thought. He had even considered committing suicide. It was simply a matter of choosing a different path when there is no road ahead. There's always another way.

Getting a job at the last moment in order to survive strengthened Anubhav's belief in god. At first, god had revealed to him the truth of life after death through the suicide of an unknown taxi driver.

'Where would the soul of the taxi driver go after his death, to heaven or to hell? The man was a devoted son and loving husband and father. He does not deserve hell. Wherever he goes, he will not be happy. If he could see the condition of his survivors, his helpless wife, poor parents and orphaned kids who didn't know yet what the word implied, his soul would only cry,' Anubhav confronted himself.

"There is no heaven or hell after death. A man's last journey ends on six feet of land. The same world is left behind for those who stay behind. Their life is the real life after death," he mumbled.

After this tragedy, god gave him a straw to grasp in order to live in a city where he wanted and work to fulfill his dreams. His belief became stronger that something else was destined for him.

Anubhav shifted to the housing society's servants' quarter and started the watchman's job. It didn't only help him financially but gave him peace of mind and he was in a position to think afresh. After all, his thoughts and dreams were the acting force that drove him, so both should flow continuously.

This low-profile job gave him a new perspective on life. He learned all the operations of the society very soon, from guarding the community to looking after each apartment's security, waking up early in the morning, turning on the water tap and washing all the cars parked there and then, switching off the lights fitted in the common area of the building.

Fauji used to come by 8 a.m. now, as he was relieved from many duties. Together, they would roam the entire society once, walk through each floor and corner of the community, the society park and parking lot and unlock the society office and recreation room, organizing everything before anybody could come, ensuring they were ready to use.

There was only one task besides sitting at the gate and monitoring the visitors after the first three hours of the busy morning schedule. Homemakers would usually call him and ask for some household help, like buying milk or vegetables. He would get a tip for it. With these tips, Anubhav used to purchase tea, samosas and other snacks for himself and Fauji.

There was ample time to talk to each other. Anubhav spoke about himself and his dreams of becoming a software engineer which impressed Fauji and he motivated him to achieve his goals one day. Once, while encouraging him, he said, "A dream does not become a reality by magic. One has to sweat in order to achieve it. It needs strong determination. It comes early for some, but it takes some time for many. The hard work is never useless, and it results in success, sooner or later."

Anubhav was curious to know why he worked as a watchman since he was a veteran. "You are a retired army personnel. You must be getting a pension. Why are you doing this watchman's job in a housing society?" he asked.

"I joined the army during the Second World War when I was eighteen and it was part of the Royal British Army. The salary was not that good, and the pension is also not like what the defence personnel are getting nowadays," the old man said.

"I have a grandson like you who is going to college. The pension is just enough to meet the basic needs of the family. This society has become my family now. I feel happy working here," he concluded.

"Did you participate in any battle during the Second World War?" Anubhav was eager to know.

"Yes, I was part of two battles. I was part of the Indian Army that invaded Hyderabad after Independence and fought the Indo-China war in 1960," said Fauji. He remembered his old days and told Anubhav wartime stories.

After listening to his stories, Anubhav felt like he was sitting in a history classroom at a university in front of a highly competent professor. Indeed, those stories were not present in any of the books. He learned many things from Fauji.

It became a daily routine for Anubhav. Although it was not a job that he wanted to continue, yet he was sincere and honest in doing each task. He was slowly trying to forget the misery and pain of more than one and a half years. He looked lively now. The signs of successive failure marked on his forehead were fading. But he never forgot his dreams for a moment, nor did he forget Ridima. She came in his dreams the previous night saying that she had joined a civil services coaching class and wanted him to join her.

Her memories were still fresh in his mind. If there was anything more beautiful than her in this sour world, it was her memories.

He had given up his dreams of becoming a software engineer in an IT company. But he didn't stop dreaming; now he had a job that made him more optimistic, and he wanted to make the best out of it.

PART 5

Dreams Come True

18

THE RESURRECTION OF DREAMS

Low self-esteem takes over the spirit when there are successive failures in life. There was a time when Anubhav became utterly hopeless and felt that his life was not worth living. Depression made him feel enormous emotional pain and loss of hope, making him unable to see any other way of dealing with the situation, other than ending his precious life.

However, he realized that only life itself could defeat adversity and overcome misfortune. He wanted to build a new season of spring and aimed to rebuild his dreams. An IT company was not for him and he was no longer interested in becoming a software engineer. The most beautiful girl he had met desired to marry a civil servant, so he decided to become a civil servant.

Destiny made him a security guard, so that he could become a civil servant. After working for a month, he counted every hour he could spare for study. He could easily manage four to six hours during the daytime to study. The society chairman had ordered him to close the main gate by 10 p.m. and lock it, so the whole night was his to study.

A study of twelve hours every day for a year was sufficient to crack the civil service exam.

Adversity must be converted into an opportunity and a man who did so, succeeded. He was determined to prepare for it, but a challenge stopped him. Acquiring the books and study material for the civil service exam required six to eight thousand rupees and Anubhav had no money.

Anubhav needed another five to six months to raise funds. By saving a thousand to fifteen hundred rupees a month, it was possible to collect enough money.

A month passed and Anubhav got his first salary of five thousand rupees. It was time to start the new campaign.

It was the first Sunday after his first paycheck and it was the only holiday for him. The chairman had advised him to rest on Sunday. Fauji was responsible for all the work except washing the cars in the morning. That was a mutual understanding between the two of them. He was free to go anywhere.

He decided to visit Abid Book Bazaar that Sunday. The Sunday book market at Abid was famous for buying second-hand books. The trail stretching from Chermas, Abid, towards the General Post Office (GPO) was filled with activity. The book bazaar stirred life into Abid, which remained closed on Sundays. With second-hand books starting at prices as low as five rupees, you never knew what you would find here. With National Geographic's hardbound magazines, Competition Success Review (CSR), India Today and other magazines dating back to the 80s and the 90s selling at one rupee per copy, magazine collectors could buy whatever they wanted. Books on advertising, political history, engineering, management and general studies were available at dirt cheap prices.

After a month of starting his job as a watchman, this old book bazaar became his favourite haunt and he began to visit it every Sunday. He would wash the cars early in the morning and wait for the nearby roadside idli-dosa shop to open.

After eating a plate of idli and vada, he would immediately go to this market and spend the whole day there looking for books and other study material required for the civil service examination. A costly book could be priced at a hundred rupees here as compared to a thousand rupees in the market. He was able to get all the books much sooner than anticipated.

The books were sold and purchased at a low price. The engineering books that he had were of no use to him now, so he cracked a deal with a shopkeeper to trade his academic books with others of his interest.

Back in the room, he counted and sorted his books which could be exchanged during the coming week's visit to Abid Book Bazaar. He found the Computer Network book he had given to Ridima, and she had returned on the last day that he had gone to drop her off at her apartment. He did not need this book and had not even opened it once after leaving her. How many times would Ridima have read it and would she ever remember him? Lost in these thoughts, he slowly turned the pages.

There was a card in between two pages of the book. Anubhav stopped turning the pages and tried to remember when he had put it there and why? He had no clue. He looked at it more closely and opened it, placing the book alongside the books to be exchanged.

It was a farewell card with a goodbye message printed on one side and a beautiful handwritten note saying, 'Raring to see you again!' on the other. A beautiful red heart was painted at the centre and the letters A and R were crafted beautifully, having a shared line between them, joining both letters together. A ten-digit mobile number was written beneath it.

He stopped as if lightning had struck his body. Why didn't he look at this after she returned the book? He had remained sunk in depression and missed her for more than a year. It produced a heartfelt impression on his susceptible mind of his negligence and rudeness to her. He couldn't stop himself and ran out of the society towards the nearest telephone booth.

He dialled the number from the telephone booth, looking at the card that was still in his hand.

"Hello."

A familiar musical voice came from the other end. But he remained silent.

"Hello..." she said again when there was no response.

Anubhav couldn't speak a single word.

Anubhav had not thought for a moment what he would say to her. He had run madly to call her when he saw the card and found her number on it.

However, his mind soon took control of his heart and emotions. His sixth sense told him of the gross injustice towards Ridima. He had not contacted her for a year. Now, he was looking for a light in his darkness filled with misery and grief.

Would he tell her that he was working as a watchman in a housing society? The questions he had glimpsed in her eyes the last time he saw her, were still in his mind, unanswered.

"Who is that?" the girl was still on the phone.

Ridima was at the other end. Her voice sounded like heaven floating down to earth, but Anubhav had made up his mind and did not say a word. The girl put down the phone, with a sound of anger.

He didn't deserve her. His guilty conscience stopped him from speaking to her again. He didn't have the morality to remind her of his name. He shredded the card in his hand so that the mobile number could not be re-read. He took a deep breath and blew the pieces of the card in the air as he came out of the telephone booth.

He was back in the room where the books had been sorted already. Ridima would remain a forgotten chapter. He had made up his mind.

Like any other Sunday, Anubhav visited the Abid Book Bazaar the following Sunday and exchanged his books. Now he was well familiar with all the shops and street vendors and knew where to find everything. It was easy to find a book and magazine of his choice without a long search, so the process of collection of the books that he needed became less time-consuming.

By noon, he had visited all the shops of interest and more than half of the day was yet left. He remembered his college friends and decided to go to Begumpet.

He reached the apartment and knocked on the door. Narendra opened the door. "Hey, Anubhav! You? Where were you for so many days, brother?" he asked, surprised. Everybody in the room rushed towards him.

Everyone was surprised as he had suddenly disappeared and had now reappeared without informing them.

"We tried to reach out to you on the mobile number you gave us, but that is unavailable continuously," said Prashant.

"Oh, that was my kin's mobile number; he has changed the sim card and number. But why were you guys trying to reach out to me? Did Four Soft call again?" he said with laughter.

"Congratulations, brother, you have been selected for AI Tech Systems," Narendra informed him and everyone started congratulating him, shaking hands and hugging him.

Anubhav was shocked and didn't believe what they were saying. He remained standing and didn't know how to react for a while. He was not expecting it. "But how do you guys know this? We had the interview for this company about four or five months ago," he said, surprised.

"Both Srini and you have been selected. Srini has got the offer letter," informed Prashant. "Didn't you check your email?"

AI Tech Systems was a small firm, and they had all taken written tests and interviewed with this company about four months ago for the post of IT Analyst. The HR department didn't declare the final result and informed them that they were withholding the positions for internal reasons.

Srini got a phone call and an email from the HR department two weeks ago as the company finally released the offer letters. Srini had accepted it and Anubhav's friends were looking for him to find out if he had accepted it as well.

"Is your internet working?" Anubhav asked.

"Yes, it's working. Check it, buddy."

Anubhav logged in to his email account after more than three months. In a short while, a smile emerged as a twinkling star in his eyes and spread to his lips. An offer letter was attached to the email he had received from the company's HR department. However, the smile lasted for a short time only.

The HR department had requested him to accept the offer letter within a couple of days and had asked to return a signed copy. He had seen it after a fortnight. Srini also joined them shortly and advised him not to worry about it. He told him to accept the offer letter and inform HR that he had no internet access and couldn't see the offer on time. Anubhav immediately replied to the email, apologizing for the delay and explaining his inability to access the email.

It was party time for all of them. Everybody appreciated Anubhav's hard work and after a long time, Anubhav shared a light moment with them. They had lunch together in a nearby tiffin house that served unlimited food for a reasonable price. Srini had gotten a CD of a newly released movie and after lunch, they watched it together on the Pentium III desktop in their room.

The day passed, and it became dark outside. Anubhav realized that his holiday was over as Fauji would be waiting for him. He took leave of his friends saying, "Friends, I need to go now. I had not informed at home where I was going."

He didn't disclose to them that he was doing a watchman's job in a housing society and staying in its servant quarter.

While on the way back to his room, he was alone once again. The storm of thoughts had started whirling in his mind. His sense of negativity and positivity flowed like waves in the ocean. His mind was not ready to accept that he could get an offer letter for a job that he had interviewed for four months ago. He had given up any hope of getting a job in his desired field and had decided to pursue another aim.

When he stopped making any effort, an offer letter had arrived for him. Was it a prank by his friends? He had seen them editing the call letters and sharing them amongst themselves. He should not get trapped in it. But he had read the offer letter and replied to the HR department. Was it from the right domain and the right person? A fishy email would have an unfamiliar domain to which he should have paid attention.

The more he thought about it, the more questions he was creating for himself. He didn't know whether to laugh or cry.

Thinking about it constantly, he reached the gate of the society but realized it only after Fauji, sitting on the chair, called out to him.

"It has been a long time since I saw you today. Where have you been, Anubhav?"

He had never been outside for such a long time.

"I have a few friends from college, so I went to visit them," he said.

"Very nice! Now relax and prepare tea so that I can leave."

Fauji liked tea prepared by Anubhav, which was the first thing he wanted to have with him when he came in the morning and before going back in the evening.

The next day in the morning, Anubhav was waiting for the clock to strike ten. He rushed to the same telephone booth outside, took out the piece of paper from his pocket on which he had written down the name and phone number of the company HR and dialled it. The phone rang and an HR staff member picked it up.

"Hello, madam. My name is Anubhav, and I got an email with an offer letter from you two weeks back," he said.

"Wait for a minute..." the HR member paused for a couple of minutes and then asked him, "are you Anubhav Gumrah?"

"Yes, madam. It's me."

"I tried to reach out to you many times, but the number you have given is always switched off. Is it the correct number to connect?" she asked.

"Actually, that is not operative now and I don't have a mobile yet. I apologize for that," he responded and tried to convince her so that this wouldn't be a reason for rejection.

"Anyway, we have an open position in our Mumbai office and we have finalized your name. Are you ready to relocate?" she asked.

The HR informed him that he had been selected four months back, but there was uncertainty over the project location, so they didn't issue the offer letter. The project had now been finalized and was about to start in their Mumbai office. The positions had also shifted over there.

It was not a prank, but a reality. The offer letter was genuine and sent by the company's HR. The smoke of uncertainty cleared and he could smile again. He wanted to share this news with someone close to him but who was there with him?

He shared everything with his fellow watchman.

"I am sorry I have to leave this job," Anubhav said to Fauji, attempting to prove that it was not his fault.

"No, you should not be sorry. I understood it the first day when you approached me. I had seen the honesty in your eyes and understood that you were in real need. Otherwise, who will work as a watchman after studying computer engineering? My blessings are with you, my child," said the older man and Anubhav's happiness increased manifold listening to him.

Anubhav's dream to join an IT company had died, and he had started dreaming of becoming a civil servant. Then again, his first dream was resurrected.

AI Tech Systems was not a known company. It was a small start-up, but a path had been paved to achieve his goal and Anubhav and his friend Srini were all set to join AI Tech Systems in the following month.

He thought of his school friend, Shibu. Shibu had studied with him till the twelfth grade. They were separated after class XII and went to different colleges and cities. Shibu got a job in HPCL, Mumbai and was living here for two years.

Anubhav looked for his mobile number and dialled him.

"Where is your office located?" Shibu asked.

"Somewhere in Andheri East."

"It is close to where I live. You note down my address and come here first. I am staying in Goregaon and you can stay with me."

Anubhav was set to live his dreams in another metro city, this time with a job in hand.

19

IN THE CITY OF DREAMS, MAYANAGARI

On 12 May 2005, Anubhav ended his struggle in Hyderabad and was ready to move to a different city once more. Fauji didn't let him work that day and commanded him to focus on his packing, though he had nothing much to pack – only a bag and a briefcase. As the clock struck 8 p.m., Fauji hired an auto-rickshaw for him.

He had arranged food and snacks from his home. Handing them over to him, he said, "Don't worry about your payment. I have talked to the society secretary, and he is ready to give your full payment today."

Anubhav hugged him and said, "I will not forget you."

Anubhav was now on the train and didn't sleep the whole night, but not because of uncertainty and fear. This time, he had many plans that he pondered over the whole night. Would he give his first salary to his mother or father to get the bulls back? How much interest might the wicked merchant have compounded? The mud house needed repairs, otherwise, it would fall during the next monsoon and how much money would be left after his grandparents' treatment? He had plans to address every misery of his family and alleviate their poverty and had countless dreams to fulfill.

It was midnight when the train reached Thane railway station, but it didn't look like night at the station. As he exited the train, auto-rickshaw drivers waiting for customers rushed towards the passengers getting off the train. Every driver wore a khaki uniform, and a token hung on the shirt's left pocket. It was no different from a scene in a Bollywood movie.

"Sir, where do you need to go?" said an old auto-rickshaw driver who approached him as he got off the train.

"Goregaon East, how much would it cost?" inquired Anubhav.

"No auto-rickshaw goes beyond Mulund Check Post. You need to take another auto-rickshaw from that point or you can take a bus," responded the old driver. Carrying Anubhav's bag, he advanced towards his auto-rickshaw that was parked outside the auto stand.

The auto-rickshaw dropped him at Mulund Check Naka bus depot, where only three or four buses stood at different stops. There were very few lights around and the place looked darker than the road across it. The staff was busy changing their duties. Anubhav approached a bus conductor who was going to board a bus which was about to leave.

"Sir, I need to go to Dindoshi. Is there any bus for it?"

"523, it's time to leave," the man answered, pointing towards a bus at the first stop. "The driver and the conductor will be there soon."

Soon, a bus driver and a conductor in khaki climbed the bus. A group of people followed them and the bus was packed in minutes. Anubhav was watching and couldn't understand from where this crowd suddenly appeared at midnight.

"Mumbai never sleeps. Is this why it is said so?" he questioned himself.

The bus had already started moving and people were still boarding it. Anubhav was sitting in a window seat, looking outside constantly, thinking about how Mumbai was different from the other two cities in which he had lived and how he was now realizing his dreams.

The streets were lit with bright yellow sodium lights on both sides, but the visibility was not much beyond the road as it was dark outside. The streets seemed comparable, but they differed from those in Pune and Hyderabad at late midnight. There was constant traffic at midnight with moving cars, autos and buses, unlike in other cities.

Anubhav was lost in his thoughts. A picture started reappearing in his mind. He had reached Pune and then Hyderabad similarly, but his dreams remained distant. Had his journey to look for a job ended or would he get stubbed one more time?

No one knew what was in the future, nor did Anubhav. He didn't even know that bus number 523 and this long route would become the most travelled road of his life.

More than an hour passed, and the bus was almost empty when it entered the Dindoshi bus depot. The conductor rang the bell twice and announced in sync with the resonance, "Dindoshi, Dindoshi… it's the last stop."

Anubhav tried to look at the hands of his wristwatch that loomed out of the darkness inside the bus. It was half-past three. He got off the bus and walked towards the auto-rickshaws standing outside the bus depot, carrying his luggage bags.

Unlike Thane railway station, the auto-rickshaw drivers were sleeping on the passenger seats and their faces were covered using a light, thin towel to protect them from the buzzing mosquitoes.

"Brother, will you go to Gokuldham?" he questioned a driver, shaking his hand.

The driver woke up immediately and sat up. Looking at his wristwatch, he said, "It will be fifteen rupees."

He took the auto-rickshaw and reached the HPCL officers' housing society in less than ten minutes. There was unbroken silence and the gates of all the buildings of the society were locked.

He tapped on the gate and a sleeping watchman woke up and opened the gate. Anubhav informed him about Shibu and the guard dialled him through the intercom in the security room. Shibu was also sleeping but knew that his friend would arrive at night. He came down quickly and took Anubhav with him.

Anubhav completed another train journey, but the journey of his dreams was yet to begin.

Anubhav was in Mumbai, ready to join AI Tech Systems. He erased the painful memories of Pune and Hyderabad from his mind and it was a new spring for him.

He took a bus from the Gokuldham bus stop outside the society and arrived at the Goregaon railway station. He was dismayed to see the long queues at the ticket counter, stopping outside the ticketing building and continuing till near the railway walkover bridge. He was scared that he would be late on the first day of office if he joined the queue but he had no choice. Shibu had advised him that the local train was the best way to reach your office on time, so he joined the line.

It took less than five minutes to get the ticket and he understood why Mumbai was called a super-fast city. He rushed towards the platform to catch the local train, which would come in a few minutes.

When the first train arrived and stopped, he couldn't catch it and got scared. The platform was crowded and packed. People raced to catch the train as it stopped and left within a few seconds. He could only watch it like a spectator. Even after the train left, the crowd didn't reduce and more people kept arriving.

He remembered the rules which Shibu had told him. He stood in one of the queues of people standing alongside the platform. The next train came in less than three minutes and he found himself inside the train. Shibu had made it clear that he needed to be at the right place and the crowd would do the job for him, pushing him inside.

Andheri was just after one station, so he didn't want to miss the chance to get down. He remembered the second rule to get off the train.

"Brother, on which side will Andheri platform come?" he inquired of a regular rider inside the packed train.

"The opposite side, join the line next to you," his co-passenger told him, pointing his head towards two queues at the opposite gate. The train was so packed that he couldn't even lift his hand.

Anubhav adjusted himself in the crowd and joined the queue before it was too late. The train stopped, and a force pushed him outside the train along the line he had joined. He was crushed, unable to breathe and about to fall.

Somehow, he managed to reach Andheri railway station on time. Srini was already waiting for him, as they had promised to meet and go to the Sampoorna Complex Andheri East office together. They hired an auto outside the railway station and requested the driver to go to the given address.

AI Tech Systems was on the fifth floor of the building. Though the entire floor belonged to it, the occupancy was not high. There were about ten employees visible there. They reached the reception desk and showed their offer letter to the lady sitting there.

"Please take a seat," she said and informed them, "Gupta sir will be coming soon."

Many empty open cubicles stretched along the floor. They pulled chairs together and sat, observing the office and other people. It had two cabins with nameplates on the doors: Shubham Gupta, Director and Shanti Gupta, Director. It did not look like an IT company.

"Looks like it's a small company," Srini said in Anubhav's ears.

After a while, a man in his mid-fifties entered the office with a briefcase. The lady at the reception greeted him and informed him about the newcomers.

"He must be Mr. Gupta," Srini whispered again.

What happened after that didn't meet their expectations. Mr. Gupta called both of them inside his cabin and welcomed them. He was polite and seemed concerned about them. Mr. Gupta inquired if they had made arrangements to live and didn't mention any allowances for initial accommodation or assistance. Then he called Monika, who they assumed was the receptionist and another employee, Hirak, sitting in the last cubicle at the corner.

"Monika, record their names and addresses in the register. Hirak will tell you guys about the work," he instructed them.

Nobody asked for any documents or forms to fill or any joining formalities like an established company. Nobody carried a badge or access card like a typical IT company employee. The lady didn't ask for their bank details and no paperwork was required. The payment system was simple: Mr. Gupta used to sign a cheque on the last day of the month for the number of days the employee was present in the office. There were no paid holidays and no benefits to discuss. There was no job orientation.

AI Tech Systems was not a software company. It was a computer and hardware supplier to multiple firms, particularly government offices that were Mr. Gupta's most prominent clients. There were seven to eight employees in Mr. Gupta's team who explored biddings and applied for tenders, except for Hirak. Hirak was a technical person who installed and maintained these computers and hardware at client locations. Shanti was Mr. Gupta's wife and used to visit the office rarely. Altogether, it looked like a family business.

Anubhav and Srini were very upset. The HR had informed them of a very different scenario. Srini was so annoyed that he decided to return to Hyderabad the next day. He even didn't talk to Mr. Gupta anymore.

At the end of business hours, everybody left the office at five in the evening. The office hours of employees matched the local train timings. Srini asked Anubhav to inform Mr. Gupta that he was going back and wouldn't come the next day. Anubhav had no choice as it was far better than the job of a watchman in a housing society and washing cars early in the morning.

Saying goodbye to Srini, Anubhav started walking towards Andheri railway station to return to Gokuldham, his new place of stay. It was a crowded sidewalk, and the road was full of cars, bikes, auto-rickshaws and buses. The traffic was almost at a standstill when he noticed the number of bus 523 in a traffic jam. He ran towards it and got on to the running bus without giving it a second thought.

"I cannot travel by local train," Anubhav said, looking at a passenger who had been observing him.

The next day, he informed Mr. Gupta that Srini had decided to leave as the job was different from what had been explained to them during the interview. Mr. Gupta told him about his plans and the future.

Supplying computers, printers and other hardware was his primary business, but he was working to provide software solutions and services. His company had recently won a multi-year IT engagement worth millions of rupees to provide software services to a major government research and development department across many cities, including Hyderabad.

"Can you see this building?" he said, pointing his finger towards the window of his cabin and showing a tall building adjacent to his office.

"I am working on renting two complete floors of it and the agreement is in the final stage. Not only this, I am also working on setting up offices in Hyderabad, Bangalore and Delhi soon. More than 200 associates will be working on this project in the next two years," he informed Anubhav and didn't stop there.

"You are going to be my first staff for this massive project. You will lead a team of more than 200 hundred people soon and have a bright future here," he said, completing his plan and disclosing why he was hiring software engineers. This project was shifted to Mumbai from his partner company in Hyderabad, where Anubhav had been interviewed. Anubhav understood why he had received the joining letter after four months of completing the interview.

Listening to the plan, Anubhav was pleased at first and satisfied. It was a start-up company and had a promising growth opportunity. However, when he was sitting alone and thought about what Mr. Gupta had told him, uncertainty clouded over the whole dream again.

He had no prior work experience. He needed training and work experience in managing a project and team. Though there was a promising future here, he could not afford the risk of failure. It would lead him to the same situation he had been in for the last two years. It was wise to use this opportunity and find a different job with an established company, which would provide him with more learning opportunities. The struggle for Anubhav was not yet over.

He completed one and a half months in AI Tech Systems and it was payday. He would get paid for the last one and a half months.

Anubhav was delighted after receiving the first paycheck. The plans were already laid on the table. He had run out of money and had waited for one and a half months for a salary. Mumbai was a much costlier city than he had anticipated. All his money ran out in just a few days, which he had hoped would be sufficient for three to four months.

Shibu had commanded that he buy a mobile phone at the earliest. They could not connect with each other when outside and most importantly, how would any recruiter communicate with him if he didn't have a number to reach out to him? Recruiters mainly connected with a candidate through the phone. Anubhav had understood its necessity and sensed that the lack of a mobile phone had drastically marginalized his job prospects in the past.

First, he wanted to shop for a mobile phone. Shibu took him to a beautiful place on Sunday – Irla, Vile Parle.

Electronic Stores was one of Mumbai's most famous home appliances and gadgets shops. It was always crowded, with many people from all over Mumbai wanting to buy gadgets. One could get a similar mobile in any other area, but the price here was unbeatable. It depended on negotiations and whether one was willing to take risks.

They picked up a mobile and its market price was about four thousand rupees, but the seller agreed to sell it for a lesser price on the condition of not issuing a bill.

"Nokia's phones are the most reliable. You will not have any issues for years. In case there are any, the cost of repair is less than the discount given here," Shibu explained to him the benefit of buying without a bill. Anubhav loved the idea and bought his first mobile, a Nokia 2600. It was not a high-end model but the first in the market to have a colour screen.

It was a day for shopping; they walked around the stores and shops and he bought a couple of shirts and pants. He didn't want anybody to say again that he came to the office wearing a school uniform. Vinod's words still reverberated in his ears.

The day was almost over, nearing dusk, with the sky growing dark in the distance. The friends had reached Bandra, roaming the malls and exploring the streets. Bandstand Promenade, the most popular walkway in the posh Mumbai suburb of Bandra, was not far away.

"Let's go to Bandstand," said Shibu, stopping an auto-rickshaw.

They reached within ten minutes. Bandra Bandstand had been immortalized in several Bollywood movies, television soaps and reality shows. Many glamorous film stars and other Bollywood celebrities had residences or bungalows around. Shibu showed him which house belonged to which star and which celebrities lived there. Anubhav's curiosity about this city was increasing.

Enjoying a prominent view of the Arabian Sea, they walked along the promenade when their eyes went to a crowd standing in front of a multistorey marvel.

"It is Mannat. Shahrukh Khan lives here," said Shibu. "The people outside it are waiting in case he might be seen."

Mannat, the bungalow of the Bollywood superstar Shahrukh Khan was lavish and a heritage building. No one was allowed to enter this gated area and guards patrolled outside. About a hundred people were standing around, hoping to get a glimpse of their favourite star.

It reminded him of Ridima. If she had been with him, he would have come here with her and stood before this bungalow until Shahrukh would have met her. After all, Shahrukh was her favourite actor.

He had made a grave mistake by not contacting her and a graver one by tearing the card into pieces. Anubhav was thinking about Ridima. He wanted to fulfill all her wishes but didn't want her to be part of his misfortune.

By remembering the past, one should not forget the happiness in the present. Anubhav learned this at a very early stage of his struggle.

"I am starving. Which is a good restaurant here?" Anubhav asked Shibu. Anubhav had got his first paycheck, so the dinner was on him and a party was due.

"Every restaurant is good here. You tell me, what would you like to have?"

"Anything that tastes good."

On the way to Bandra railway station, they went to Persian Darbar, a restaurant serving traditional cuisine.

Two days passed and Anubhav got his mobile. He was eager to make calls to his well-wishers and wanted to share his number with them and tell them that he had also bought a mobile phone. He called his uncle living in Pune, his kin and every other well-wisher.

He tried calling Fauji in Hyderabad many times, but all the calls went unanswered. While leaving Hyderabad, Fauji had promised to deposit his outstanding payment to his bank account. He had shared his bank details with him, but had no clue about what had happened to his promise. Did he cheat him? He was money-minded. He used to take half of the money Anubhav made by washing cars in the society.

To clear up the confusion in his mind, he called Mr. Rao, the society chairman.

"Fauji is no more. He had a cardiac attack twenty days back and lost his life before he could be admitted to the hospital," informed Mr. Rao.

It shocked Anubhav. He had been with Fauji about two months back and such an event was beyond belief. Life could not be more unpredictable than this.

Mr. Rao continued speaking on the phone and repeatedly requested him to return to Hyderabad and look after the society. They still needed to hire a guard and were urgently looking for one.

"I will pay you double of what I paid before and give you a railway ticket to Hyderabad from your village. You just come here," promised Mr. Rao on the phone.

"I am sorry, sir. I can't come back," returned Anubhav. "But please do me a favour. Give my outstanding payment to his family."

"Thank you very much, Anubhav. You are a kind person. His family needs support, and the society is raising funds for his family. Your help is appreciated. But why can't you come back? Let me know if you want anything else. Tell me your concern."

Anubhav put down the phone. Mr. Rao didn't know that he was an engineering graduate and wanted to become a software engineer in an IT company. He had not told anyone there except Fauji about it.

He was sad for the first time since he came to Mumbai. Fauji had become his good friend and looked after him like a guardian. He asked him daily if he had had lunch or dinner and what he had eaten and occasionally carried food from his home for him. He was a companion in his struggle and helped him when he was in dire need. Fauji's death was a huge loss to him.

20

DREAMS COME TRUE

Anubhav's misfortune began to subside. Though he was not working in a well-known IT company as he had wanted, he had a job and expected a good project to begin. There was nothing to learn or much work to perform, but there was hope.

Mr. Gupta attended meetings with the client frequently and he included Anubhav in them. Mr. Gupta once visited Hyderabad at the client's office and asked Anubhav to accompany him. He introduced Anubhav as the principal engineer of his company and it was Anubhav who was supposed to attend such meetings in the future. Anubhav noted that it would be a big project, and a blueprint was ready, but no dates had been decided to start it full-fledged.

Most of the time, he had no work, so Mr. Gupta instructed Hirak to offload some of his work to Anubhav. He travelled to his client locations across Mumbai to perform desktop or printer installations, but this was also limited to hardly a couple of times a week. Most of the time, Anubhav was free, which allowed him to explore other job opportunities.

He started getting interview calls on his mobile, but he had grown wise enough to enquire about projects, roles and responsibilities, unlike before. He was not desperate like before to join any job.

One day after lunch, he was resting in his cubicle and trying to keep himself awake without any work when he got a phone call from a recruiter. It was from the HR department of Patni Computers Systems (PCS). Patni was one of Mumbai's most reputed software companies. He had applied there in the past and his resume had been shortlisted. The recruiter wanted to talk to him.

He requested to hold the call for a minute and ran outside the office to the building gallery, where nobody was present.

"Yes, madam," he said in a hushed voice. "I am looking for a change and we can talk now."

"Your profile is shortlisted for the position of software engineer. You need to come for the written test this Saturday. I am going to email the invitation and details," she said.

"Yes, madam, I am available," answered Anubhav promptly and his eyes started shining, listening to her.

He got the email from the HR department fifteen minutes after the call. The email had a venue and test details on it. The test location was one of the Patni offices in Andheri, near the AI Tech Systems office. Anubhav took a printout of the email, hiding it from everybody in the office.

Saturday was a working day for him and presence was compulsory to mark attendance. Otherwise, there was a pay cut for a lost day. He didn't want to miss any payment from his paycheck, so he planned to attend the office late and had an excuse ready.

Anubhav arrived at the Patni office the following Saturday instead of going to AI Tech Systems.

It was a computer-based test, and the arrangements were already made. The HR member shared log-in credentials with him and he was ready to start the test soon after reaching there.

It was an easy enough test and Anubhav completed it before time. After completing the formalities, he was on the way back to his office, but the question paper was still running through his mind like a printing machine. Anubhav recalled all the questions and was confident that all his answers were correct. However, he had this confidence in the past as well and had failed so far.

Was there an upper cut-off and would he get disqualified for scoring more than the upper limit? Achieving above a limit or a hundred percent could be considered a case of cheating or knowing the question paper in advance. Why not attempt a few questions wrong intentionally so as not to be trapped in such an evaluation? He was in a dilemma and it reminded him of the famous teaching of the Bhagavad Gita:

'You can do only your duties, but the outcome is out of your control. So, never think that you are the reason for the outcome. Do your duties without being attached to the outcome.'

He stopped believing in a good or bad test.

When he reached the office, it was almost lunchtime and everybody, including Mr. Gupta, was present. He had an excuse handy that he had thought of before. He apologized for being late and informed him that he needed to visit the bank for an unavoidable money order.

"No problem, keep me informed in advance in the future," said Mr. Gupta, who didn't bother about it.

Back in the room at Gokuldham, Anubhav and Shibu were having dinner together when he told him about his test and how he had dodged Mr. Gupta.

"What! Are you crazy?" said Shibu, laughing uncontrollably. "Didn't you find any other excuse?"

"Why?" asked Anubhav, puzzled as to why his friend was laughing at him. "What is wrong with it?"

"It was a bank holiday today. Hopefully, your boss is stupid like you."

Anubhav was shaken, realizing his blunder. He couldn't say anything but was optimistic that Mr. Gupta hadn't caught his lie and was possibly unaware of it.

Anubhav was not good at lying. He had faked a call letter in Hyderabad and had been caught red-handed. His first excuse in the office was a blunder.

Every goal can be achieved by following the truth. Anubhav decided to take a holiday the next time, though he would not be paid for that day. He needed to pay for it if he wanted a good opportunity.

Anubhav anticipated qualifying for the written test, so he regularly checked his email twice or thrice a day. He had saved the HR number on his mobile and checked the missed call entries every hour to ensure any call didn't go unanswered. But two weeks passed, and he didn't receive any communication. A computer-based test should take little time to generate results, so doubt started racing in his mind. He thought of following up with the company but was not hopeful of a positive reply, so he gave up hope. Not being selected in a test was no longer a matter of grief as he had a job.

He was sitting in his cubicle doing some work when the phone rang suddenly. He looked at the caller id, which was that of the HR department at Patni Computers. He picked up the call and ran towards the gallery outside the office, where no one could hear him speaking.

Before anyone could address him from the other end, he said promptly, holding his breath, "Good afternoon, madam. Anubhav, speaking here."

"Hi, Anubhav. This is Sandra," she said over the phone. "How are you doing today?"

"I have been waiting for your call for the last two weeks."

"Congratulations, you have cleared the first round. Sorry about the delay. It took some time to arrange for an interview panel. The interviews are scheduled for next week, Monday to Friday," she informed him and requested his availability. "Which day suits you?"

Anubhav jumped joyfully listening to this and said, "Monday is fine. Though I can make it any day," he said. He wanted to go the same day but had to wait till next week.

"Ok, I will book a slot for you on Monday. You must be here by 10 a.m., but please ensure you have enough time. The process is lengthy and it will take time. We will wrap the entire process the same day."

The smile on a face reveals what is inside the heart. Anubhav wanted to avoid encountering anyone, so he went outside the building to get snacks and tea. He could smile and laugh here as much as he wanted without anyone noticing and asking why.

The following Monday, Anubhav reached the Akruti building of Patni Computers at the scheduled time. This time, he had already informed Mr. Gupta that he would be out on Monday.

Patni office was easily distinguished by its unique buses parked along both sides of the road reaching the office building. Patni was one of the most reputed companies and working there was prestigious. He was confident that he would make it and it would not be like before. It would be unlike the other companies where he had been interviewed in the past.

He reached the fourth floor. There were already about twenty people in the waiting area of the reception lobby and there was no place left to sit. He could easily guess that the crowd included candidates who had qualified for the first round and had come for the next level. He also joined the group that was discussing the interview and their stories.

He had waited around half an hour when a tall lady wearing spectacles with thick lenses came out of the door near the reception area. She requested them to move inside and instructed that their visitor card should always be visible. When everybody went inside, she closed the door and started walking straight towards a big meeting room and the crowd followed her.

"My name is Sandra and I am the recruitment coordinator," she declared once everybody entered the meeting room. Two big TVs and a projector were stationed on both sides of the meeting room. Its walls looked like a whiteboard where you could write anywhere and a marker stand was stuck with a dozen erasable markers. What is the use of it? Anubhav observed the entire room quickly. A teapot, a pack of water bottles, sodas, snacks and biscuits were in one corner of the room as was a small refrigerator.

She handed over an information sheet to everyone and asked them to fill it out while explaining the interview process. It would start with a technical round and there would be two more for those who qualified.

She collected the information sheet, requested them to be seated and informed them that the interviewers would call out their names. The tea and snacks were for them and they could help themselves anytime.

There were multiple interview panels, and they called four of the candidates first. Anubhav waited an hour before a young man called him, a card from Patni Computers hanging on his neck. He took Anubhav to another small meeting room where only four to five people could sit. Another person was already sitting there, and he was a part of the two-member panel to interview him.

The interview went smoothly and Anubhav answered every question flawlessly. More than thirty minutes had passed when one of them asked about his current project and its architecture.

Anubhav suddenly lost his rhythm. He paused first and couldn't answer the question well. He had a project but no architecture as it did not exist and it was only on paper. But he explained it in broken words.

When Sandra returned, the first round of interviews had ended and Anubhav sat in the meeting room with the other candidates. The clock's hand was about to touch 1 p.m. She looked at a paper in her hand and started announcing names without giving any instructions.

"Pankaj Singh, Nikhil Jadhav, Sayantani Sen... and Anubhav Gumrah."

Anubhav's name was announced sixth on the list, but everyone was puzzled. Was it a selection list or a rejection one that she had read out? Everyone remained silent.

Sandra didn't mean to create suspense and continued to speak. "These are the eight candidates who have qualified and need to stay for the next round. Sorry about the others. You can apply again after six months."

Hearing his name on the list, Anubhav sighed in relief as the question about the current project design had caused him deep concern.

Then, she turned to another portion of the paper in her hand. It was a small booklet with some tickets printed on it. She pulled a piece off it and distributed it to all the selected candidates.

"This is the food coupon. The canteen is on the top floor. I should see you here again by 2 p.m.," said Sandra, revealing the mystery behind the tickets in the booklet that she distributed to them.

He went to the tenth floor. The entire floor was full of rows of dining tables and there were multiple caterers. But there was a specific counter that accepted the food coupons. When he gave the voucher to the attendant standing there, the attendant handed over a plate and requested him to proceed to the buffet section. Anubhav's eyes were on the ambience and the crowd.

The following two rounds of the interview were going to decide his future. Would he lunch here again or at the roadside food stall outside AI Tech Systems? Many thoughts were running through his mind and he was still nervous about the remaining interview.

He finished his food quickly and returned to the fourth floor to the same meeting room. No other candidates were back by that time. Anubhav looked at his watch and it was only 1:30 p.m. He was alone in the meeting room and the door was closed. He walked towards the wall where the markers were placed and took out one of the markers. He ran it on a wall, which was a whiteboard. He filled it with the painting that was in his mind, a picture of a homeless boy looking at a sunset at a shore and a colourful rainbow above the sky. As he completed drawing, the other candidates came back one after another and Sandra came back precisely at 2:00 p.m.

First, she called Pankaj and took him to another meeting room, where another lady sat with her. She was the HR manager and was there to take the next round of interviews along with her. She called the candidates one after another in the same sequence in which she had announced the names.

Anubhav was called sixth and the interview of all eight candidates was over by 4:30 p.m. Then Sandra entered the room a third time.

"Sayantani Sen, Pankaj Singh, Anubhav Gumrah, Nirav Jain and Sachin Chawan – the five of you need to wait for the final round to meet Mr. Sunil Kulkarni," she announced quickly and left the room.

"Congratulations, you have been selected," said Nikhil, sitting beside Anubhav and congratulating him before leaving the room.

"There is one more round to go," said Anubhav.

"You no longer need to worry. You have made it. Sunil is the HR head, and you are selected if you are going to see him," said Nikhil, as though he knew about it, before leaving the room with the other two. "He is there to sign the offer letter."

Meanwhile, a waiter came to the room and asked if they wanted snacks, tea or coffee. Thirst and hunger were far away from Anubhav in this situation, but he wanted to enjoy this moment. He ordered a grilled sandwich and a filtered coffee.

Nikhil was correct. Hardly anyone spent more than fifteen minutes with Sunil. Sunil was a very senior person and was there to complete the formalities and sign the offer letter. When it was Anubhav's term, he only asked, "Tell me about yourself in brief."

While Anubhav was answering, Sunil kept making entries on his laptop. He hardly looked at Anubhav, though he constantly interacted and then said, "I am offering you a yearly package of Rs. 3,20,000/- per year. You will enjoy all the company benefits. Sandra will inform you about this in detail. It's a critical position and you must join at the earliest."

Anubhav was listening to him carefully.

"Congratulations on joining Team Patni."

Anubhav didn't believe his ears. Had he heard correctly? He wanted Sunil to repeat what he had said at the end but couldn't gather the courage to ask.

Anubhav returned to the meeting room where the other four candidates sat, but his mind was completely blank. He could not react and his mind was not ready to accept that his dream had come true.

It took more than an hour before Sandra came back. This time, she was carrying a bunch of papers in her hand.

"Congratulations to all of you. You have been selected," said Sandra. "I have your offer letters ready."

She gave them two copies of the offer letters and requested them to review them thoroughly and return a signed copy of them. The second copy was for them. Then she explained the policies and the formalities of joining.

It was 7 p.m. The interview formalities were completed and everybody was free to leave. Anubhav came outside the HR block to the lobby towards the lift. He opened the offer letter again which was still in his hand. He read it multiple times, again and again. He was visualizing his dreams in every word of it. An offer letter was in his hand. It was not just a piece of paper. It was a miracle; happened after countless struggles. His dream had finally come true.

It was raining when he reached the ground floor and outside the office. The company buses stood in line and waited outside in the rain. The employees used umbrellas to protect themselves from the rain and helped each other. Anubhav needed to wait to board the company bus. He was yet to become an employee.

It was the rainy season, so he used to carry a few plastic bags with him, one to cover his mobile, one for his wallet and a bigger one to protect the papers inside his shoulder bag. He took out all the bags and wrapped his mobile and wallet first, then all the documents inside the backpack in the bigger polythene, including the offer letter. It was precious and must not get wet.

He placed everything in his backpack to secure them from the rain. He occupied a corner near the entrance of the building, waiting for the rain to stop. Employees were leaving the office and boarding buses that were standing outside. He was enjoying the scene and dreaming of being among them soon.

The clouds in the sky got darker, and it started raining more heavily. The gusty wind was blowing outside, but there was a different storm in Anubhav's mind. Every struggle he had gone through was passing through his mind and flashing before his eyes like a flame of fire. His heart was flooded with emotions and he wanted to cry out loud. The dam of feelings inside him was to break.

The gusts of wind called out to him to swing with them and the rain invited him to embrace it and wash away all his sorrow. The clouds in his mind and heart were larger than those in the sky.

A multitude of emotions rose up inside him. Swiftly, Anubhav ran outside the building towards the road and went as fast as he could. He was crying, and every tear mingled with the loud raindrops striking his face. He wanted to cry with happiness.

He ran in the rain so that no one could see him crying. He wanted to scream in the rainfall with every flash of lightning through the clouds.

Bus stops came and passed, but he didn't stop. He didn't want to take a bus, he was riding on the horses of his dreams. The teardrops in his eyes were not willing to stop. His feet lifted off the ground as he talked to the skies. He couldn't see people, bikes, cars, buses or anything on the road. Nothing on the way was visible to him; he was running like a mad man on the street, looking up at the sky and in the seventh heaven of delight. His tears got lost in the falling raindrops.

Since he had got this offer, he must leave AI Tech Systems now. As soon as this thought came to his mind, he started crying even more. But this time, they were tears of sadness. Though he had spent only six months here, it had given him a monthly earning, enough to live in Mumbai and have peace of mind. It was a job that had raised his hopes high. Here, his dreams had come true.

He knew Patni was not his final destination and wondered how many companies he would leave and join. But he was sure that he would never feel the same way as that day, nor would it hurt him to think of leaving any company as it did to leave AI Tech Systems.

With a mix of emotions, tears of happiness and sadness together, he kept walking like a mad man. He hit a tree, sometimes a pole or avoided falling into a pothole. His steps were changing with the speed of the rain. So were the tears in his eyes – increasing and decreasing with the number of raindrops.

The rain stopped after half an hour and the storm in his mind settled as well. He was halfway to Gokuldham towards his room but didn't look for a bus. He wanted to walk alone till the end of the road.

The street lights went on and the road started sparkling, reflecting the water flowing on it.

He didn't stop walking. The trees on the way were drenched and their leaves hummed with him. He was bouncing and splashing like a toddler, enjoying the nightfall and water logging on the way.

Anubhav had spent about six months in Mumbai, the Mayanagari, and had got a job he had always dreamt of. He left AI Tech Systems with a heavy heart and joined Patni Computer Systems.

He started with a significant project of high visibility. The client was in Silicon Valley, CA and it was his first opportunity to prove himself. He started working on the project, giving more than a hundred percent.

After a few days of joining Patni, he shifted near Mulund and started living with friends working on the same project. Though he changed his job, the route remained the same. Bus number 523 remained a part of his daily routine. He used to travel to the office in the same bus at Mulund Check Naka bus stop. Every morning, it reminded him of his first day in Mumbai.

His first project ended in about a year and was a grand success for the company. A project party was organized to celebrate its success at a five-star hotel, Hotel Leela, near the airport.

Anubhav had visited a five-star hotel in Hyderabad only once for an interview and the experience was terrible. He had not forgotten how he had run out of it. The nightmare was over and a new day had dawned and it would be his first party. He was well dressed. His brilliant tie, shining pin and glittering rings were striking in their effect. His new shoes were shining.

The stage was ready and the prize ceremony was going on. Anubhav heard his name; and the hall erupted with applause.

When he reached the stage, the project director handed him a souvenir and a certificate and said to everyone, "You are a rock star. I want to see you onsite."

The party had started and people were drinking and dancing. He also approached the bar with his friends but didn't know the name of any drink. He had never had alcohol before.

"Same," he said to the bar attendant, pointing towards a lady colleague who had ordered a drink before him, thinking it must be without alcohol or a light one.

He waited some time to ensure that he didn't lose balance, but the music was tempting. He jumped on the floor and danced like never before. Everyone stopped dancing and started watching Anubhav dancing all over the floor.

Success is like a tree planted in the conscience. Anubhav planted the seed of a dream in his mind and struggled to grow it. Time had buried it once, but he did not let it dry. Anubhav's dedication and hard work were recognized. The management and client were happy with him and wanted him to lead from the front. Soon after, he was assigned a new responsibility, this time on the client's side. He was ready to fly onsite to Silicon Valley, California.

Anubhav had not boarded an airplane before and it would be his first plane journey as well as international flight. He opened the envelope of Air Korea that the travel department gave him for a flight from Mumbai Chhatrapati Shivaji International Airport to San Francisco, CA on 29th July 2007. He carefully looked at the ticket and remembered the day and month. It was the same day and month he had started from Satna to Pune on a train, four years back. Once more, numerology and astrology knocked on the door of his mind, but with an added note:

Every struggle is a success, and every success has its roots in a dream.